150 Best Meals in a Jar

Salads, Soups, Rice Bowls & More

Tanya Linton

Robert
ROSE

Design and production: Kevin Cockburn/
  PageWave Graphics Inc.
Editor: Sue Sumeraj
Recipe editor: Jennifer MacKenzie
Proofreader: Kelly Jones
Indexer: Gillian Watts

Photographer: Colin Erricson
Associate photographer: Matt Johannsson
Food stylist: Michael Elliott
Prop stylist: Charlene Erricson

Additional photographs: Mosaic #1: Shelled Walnuts © istockphoto.com/FreezeFrameStudio; Boiled Eggs © istockphoto.com/creacart; Sliced Chicken © istockphoto.com/MentalArt; Fresh Mozzarella © istockphoto.com/tycoon751; Ruccola © istockphoto.com/humbak; Black Olives © istockphoto.com/Mariha-kitchen; Microgreens © istockphoto.com/bhofack2; Grilled Halibut © istockphoto.com/LauriPatterson; Strawberries © istockphoto.com/karandaev; Shallots © istockphoto.com/VMJones; Cherry Tomatoes © istockphoto.com/xxmmxx; Corn © istockphoto.com/robynmac; Snow Peas © istockphoto.com/Victorburnside; White Mushrooms © istockphoto.com/lisaaMC; Potatoes © istockphoto.com/StephM2506; Carrots © istockphoto.com/AndreaKuipers; Creamy Dill Dressing © istockphoto.com/ajafoto; Avocado Dressing © istockphoto.com/cobraphoto; Thousand Island Dressing © istockphoto.com/ivanmateev; Vinaigrette © istockphoto.com/razmarinka; Chocolate Protein Smoothie © shutterstock.com/SherSor; Hummus Snack Pack © istockphoto.com/Karcich; Squash Soup with Yogurt and Chives © istockphoto.com/sf_foodphoto; Basic Vinaigrette © istockphoto.com/VeselovaElena; Ranch and Avocado Lime Dressings © istockphoto.com/LauriPatterson; Teensy Apple Crisps © istockphoto.com/edoneil; Mosaic #2: Cheese © istockphoto.com/vaskoni; Shrimps © istockphoto.com/joannatkaczuk; Lemons © istockphoto.com/Dimitris66; Tofu © istockphoto.com/bhofack2; Leafy Greens © istockphoto.com/ROTTSTRA; Oranges © istockphoto.com/JohnArcher; Avocado © istockphoto.com/jmalov; Sliced Steak © istockphoto.com/LauriPatterson; Red Onions © istockphoto.com/harmpeti; Asparagus © istockphoto.com/Stieglitz; Red Bell Peppers © istockphoto.com/xavierarnau; Spinach © istockphoto.com/Kativ; Rice © istockphoto.com/FooDFactory; Radishes © istockphoto.com/MKucova; Spaghetti Pasta © istockphoto.com/InaTs; Eggplants © istockphoto.com/P_Wei; Chicken Broth © istockphoto.com/Photosiber; Tomato Sauce © istockphoto.com/LauriPatterson; Soy Sauce © istockphoto.com/shingopix; Hummus © istockphoto.com/sf_foodphoto; Chapter opener image: @ istockphoto.com/mm88, Jar illustration: @ istockphoto.com/Big_Ryan

Cover image: Classic Cobb Salad (page 114), Shrimp Cocktail Salad (page 110) and Santa Fe Rice Bowl (page 125)

The publisher gratefully acknowledges the financial support of our publishing program by the Government of Canada through the Canada Book Fund.

Published by Robert Rose Inc.
120 Eglinton Avenue East, Suite 800, Toronto, Ontario, Canada M4P 1E2
Tel: (416) 322-6552 Fax: (416) 322-6936
www.robertrose.ca

Printed and bound in Canada

1 2 3 4 5 6 7 8 9 MI 24 23 22 21 20 19 18 17 16

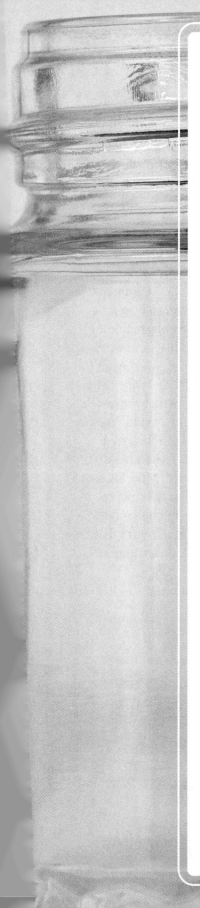

Contents

Acknowledgments

I never thought my obsession with mason jar meals would turn into a book, and for that I'm grateful to Bob Dees and the Robert Rose team, including Marion Jarkovich and Martine Quibell. Thank you to my editor, Sue Sumeraj, who edited with skill and patience and offered ideas that made the book better. It was such a treat to work with Jennifer MacKenzie, an old friend and colleague, who put her amazing knowledge of food and recipe testing into this book. Thanks also to Kevin Cockburn, who worked his magic on the design of the cookbook.

When I took on the writing of this book, I was simultaneously producing a big lifestyle television show. I had daily panic attacks about my workload, and I flat out wouldn't have been able to write this book without the help of a few people. My sister, Sam Linton, who is the best salad dressing maker I know, offered to test many of the dressing recipes and loaned her culinary style to that chapter. My mother, Marilyn Linton, who inspired me to want to be in the kitchen, helped me create some of the delicious soups. My very dear friend Mildred Piad influenced many of the noodle recipes and used her mean chopping skills to keep the testing in order. And my dad, Doug Linton, did everything a dad should do to keep me laughing throughout it all.

Finally, I need to thank all of my Sheerin boys. My three young sons were unbelievably patient with the computer work and kitchen testing, and my lack of attention to them. Thanks to Eddie for being so proud that his mom wrote a cookbook. Thank you to Murray for eating everything, even the recipes with odd combinations. I love that you have a passion for food. Thanks even to Frankie for trying nothing and thinking that everything tastes yucky. And a huge thank you to my husband, Mike Sheerin. He was the number one consumer of these dishes, and although he would prefer to eat the same lunch every day, he tried them all, except for anything with blue cheese or olives.

Introduction

I'm a salad girl. I always have been. My Ukrainian grandfather, Charlie Mazur, made the most boring garden salad, which he served to us at our family Sunday night dinners, but to me it was magical. He used a simple base of crunchy iceberg lettuce, but it was his toppings of cucumbers, carrots and tomatoes, pulled fresh from his little backyard garden, that made it shine. He then carefully crafted a dressing of vegetable oil, white vinegar, a pinch of sugar, chopped green onions and his secret ingredient (which my sister and I had to pull out of him): a pinch of chicken bouillon, for a pop of flavor. He served the same salad for years, and I never tired of it.

If that wasn't enough to cement my passion for vegetables, my mother introduced me to the art of making a meal out of a salad. She would wow me with her creations, always managing to turn nuts, cheese, designer lettuces, local fresh vegetables and the finest olive oils and vinegars into a drool-worthy dinner.

As a result of these influences, creating big flavors out of a few ingredients is my thing. But it wasn't until recently, when I left my corporate job and joined forces with my husband, that I realized just how much of a thing it was. My old job was in an ideal location in the center of the city, with every lunch option available to me. My new spot offered a lot less in the choice department, so I started thinking about meals that would be easy to make and easy to take to work. I soon tired of the basics and turned to social media to get some portable meal ideas. And that's when I discovered the mason jar meal. Type "mason jar recipes" into Pinterest or Instagram — you'll be amazed at their popularity and the variety you'll find.

At first, it was the pretty pictures that caught my eye, but as I started researching mason jar meals, it was the theory behind them that got me intrigued. In the past, I would run around in the morning making lunches for my three boys and a quick salad or pasta for me. But now I was learning that, if you organize yourself and prepare each meal accordingly, you can have two to three days' worth of crisp salads and delicious meals lined up in a row in your refrigerator. You just have to grab and go. It was life-changing! From then on, I was hooked on creating, testing and styling foods in mason jars.

Once you start using mason jars, you realize how versatile they can be. I started with salads, but soon experimented with creating breakfasts, snacks, pastas, rice bowls, heartier meals and desserts that could be prepared, transported and eaten in a mason jar. I discovered how to layer pasta, paella and polenta. I turned leftovers into a portable lunch. I experimented with the classics, like mac and cheese, shepherd's pie and lasagna to figure out how to deconstruct them and layer them in a mason jar.

I hope this book gives you some great recipes to add to your daily repertoire, but more important, I hope it encourages you to experiment in the kitchen. The beauty of a mason jar meal is that almost anything works. Use these recipes as guides or inspiration for your own creations. And don't be afraid to work with what you have on hand. Some of my favorite recipes are combinations that I made with leftovers in the fridge. Enjoy!

Mason Jar Basics

The mason jar, which was invented in 1858 by John Landis Mason, a New Jersey native, was a game changer in the world of food preservation. Experimenting with heat-based canning, pioneered by a Frenchman in 1806, Mason created a heatproof jar with a ribbed neck and a screw-on cap that created an airtight seal. His invention made it possible to eat green beans, apples and peaches in January.

In the decades since, canning has gone through stages of being popular, not-so-popular and popular again. The latest resurgence is less about canning and more about alternative uses for mason jars: they can be used to organize your office clutter, create crafts, store dry goods in your pantry and, of course, hold layered salads and other meals.

The storage time for a meal in a mason jar is nowhere near as long as the shelf life of a preserved vegetable, but most of the meals in this book can be stored for two to three days in the refrigerator. The freshness of the meal is reliant on layering, with dressings or sauces on the bottom, followed by heavier ingredients in the middle and lighter or more fragile items on top.

Equipment You'll Need

The main equipment you'll need, of course, is mason jars, but there are a few other items, such as a funnel and tongs, that will make packing your jars easier.

Mason Jar Pluses

There aren't a lot of downsides to using mason jars to store your food, but there are a ton of pluses. It's true that you will have to invest in a few different jar sizes, but the benefits for the minimal cost outlay are truly great.

- *Glass is trendy.* In the wake of consumer reports about the potential health risks associated with plastic containers, you can feel confident about the safety of storing and reheating your food in glass containers. Toss out all those plastic containers to make room for glass mason jars. They can be reused indefinitely, they can be cleaned in the dishwasher, and they go from refrigerator to microwave seamlessly (just remove the lid before microwaving).
- *Meal assembly is efficient.* If you prepare all of your ingredients in advance, you can pack your meals into jars assembly line–style.
- *Your food will stay fresh.* As long as you layer your meals properly and seal the lid tightly, your meals will stay fresh for several days.
- *Cleanup is a snap.* Mason jars are easy to wash at work or at home. If you use a dishwasher, they'll be fully sterilized, too.
- *Portion control is easy.* Mason jars allow you to manage the size of your meals, which can be challenging if you regularly go out for lunch. Most fast foods are not portion-controlled, so even if you order something healthy, the odds are good that you are eating too much food.

Mason Jars

To get started, you'll need mason jars in a few different sizes. Go for wide-mouthed jars if you can find them — they make both assembly and eating meals straight from the jar much easier.

- **1-quart (1 L) jars:** If you buy only one jar size, buy this one. I use these jars the most. All of my salads and rice bowls are prepared in a quart jar, as are some of the soups and a few of the hearty meals.
- **1-pint (500 mL) jars:** Pint jars are good for meals where a smaller portion is desirable. Many of the breakfasts and hearty meals use this size jar. They can also be used to store large batches of dressing.
- **8-oz (250 mL) jars:** These jars — often called half-pint jars — are great for making salad dressings. Just add the ingredients, seal the lid and shake them up, then store in the refrigerator. This is also the perfect portion size for some snacks and desserts.
- **4-oz (125 mL) jars:** Since they hold only a very small portion, you'll get the least use out of these jars, but they're an excellent way to transport certain dips, snacks and desserts, or any ingredient you want to keep separate from your main meal.

Lids

You can use the two-piece metal lids and rings that come with the jars to seal them. Both the flat lid pieces and rings can be reused for meals in jars (unlike for canning, where only new lids should be used), but do check to make sure there is no sign of rust, dents or bends, which can prevent a tight seal. Another alternative is to buy plastic storage lids, which are handy for non-canning uses of mason jars.

Canning Funnel

If you don't have wide-mouth jars — or even if you do — a canning funnel is a great asset when you're pouring dressing or other sauces into the jar. It helps you avoid splashing the sides of the jar (for maximum freshness, you don't want dressing to touch the other ingredients, particularly lettuce, until you're ready to serve).

Kitchen Tongs

Tongs are skinny enough to reach deep into the jar, helping you to arrange the ingredients in layers.

Serving Spoon

The back of a serving spoon is ideal for pressing layers down to make more room for other ingredients.

Hygiene, Refrigeration and Food Safety

Keep your mason jars scrupulously clean and sanitized by washing them in the dishwasher. If you don't have a dishwasher, wash them in hot soapy water and rinse with hot water. Before preparing any of the recipes, be sure to wash your hands thoroughly with hot soapy water and rinse with warm water. You can also use disposable latex gloves or reusable gloves that are solely used for food (not cleaning) when prepping the meals to ensure the utmost care in regard to hygiene and food safety.

All vegetables and fruits should be properly cleaned before they are packed into the jar. All hot items should be cooled to room temperature before the lid is sealed and the jar is placed in the refrigerator.

These recipes are not meant to be stored for a long period of time or to be stored outside the refrigerator.

Mason Jar Salad Assembly

1. Start by pouring or spooning the dressing into the bottom of the jar. Be sure to wipe down any splashes on the side of the jar, especially if you're not using a funnel.
2. Next, add layers of firmer vegetables, such as radishes, cucumbers, carrots or celery, or anything that will remain firm in dressing or will benefit from being marinated for a few days, like onions, beans or tomatoes. Pack the layers in tightly.
3. Continue layering softer ingredients, such as corn, peas, squash or green onions.
4. Pack in the lettuce or other greens. Don't be shy — press the leaves in tightly. After a few days, lightly packed lettuce will settle, leaving a gap at the top of the jar. The less air in the jar, the crisper your salad will stay.
5. Top with your protein, such as chicken, egg, nuts or cheese. (You can always pack it separately, if necessary, but it works perfectly tightly packed at the top of the jar.) Be sure to leave as little air in the jar as possible.
6. Seal the jar and refrigerate as directed in the recipe.
7. When ready to serve, turn the jar upside down in a bowl and let the dressing coat the salad. Enjoy!

Mason Jar Meal Assembly

1. Start by pouring or spooning the sauce into the bottom of the jar. Be sure to wipe down any splashes on the side of the jar, especially if you're not using a funnel.
2. Add hearty ingredients that can withstand sitting in sauce, such as pasta, rice or firm vegetables.
3. Continue adding layers of ingredients, working from heavy to light, with fragile items such as cheese and eggs on top.
4. Seal the jar and refrigerate as directed in the recipe.
5. When ready to serve, remove the lid and, if applicable, reheat in the microwave as directed. Enjoy!

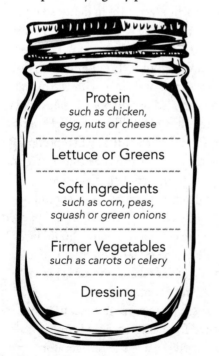

Protein
such as chicken, egg, nuts or cheese

Lettuce or Greens

Soft Ingredients
such as corn, peas, squash or green onions

Firmer Vegetables
such as carrots or celery

Dressing

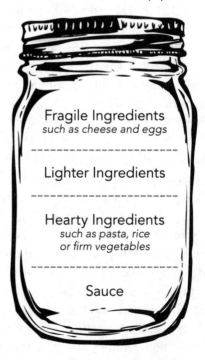

Fragile Ingredients
such as cheese and eggs

Lighter Ingredients

Hearty Ingredients
such as pasta, rice or firm vegetables

Sauce

Substituting Ingredients

I wrote this cookbook because I was looking for inspiration for my own meals. As much as I love to follow a good recipe (and there are some great ones in this book), I also love to encourage people to experiment. Everyone has a cooking style. Mine is more rustic and on-the-fly. If a recipe calls for something I don't have on hand, I soldier on with a different ingredient. If I love the pasta but hate the sauce, I switch it up with a sauce I do like. For my husband, who hates blue cheese, I substitute another cheese.

My point is, you can follow the recipes exactly as they're written and that's great, but I hope you will experiment with ingredient substitutions and get ideas for your own versions of these meals.

Dos and Don'ts for the Perfect Meal in a Jar

- *Do* prep all of your ingredients ahead of time so assembly is a breeze.
- *Do* use a vinaigrette as your dressing. Vinaigrettes hold up the best and don't separate over time.
- *Do* put wet ingredients (such as roasted peppers packed in water or oil) on the bottom, in the dressing.
- *Do* use a paper towel to blot any splashes of liquid off the sides of the jar.
- *Do* layer harder vegetables on the bottom and lighter fare on top.
- *Do* toss avocados and apples with lemon juice before adding them to the salad. This will help prevent them from browning.
- *Do* pack the protein tightly on top so there is no room left in the jar.
- *Do* use a small round of parchment paper to separate moist proteins (such as eggs and cheese) from softer vegetables.
- *Do* pack the ingredients in tightly. Air is the enemy when it comes to keeping food fresh for a few days.
- *Do* heat rice bowls, pasta salads and hearty meals in the microwave, but remember to take off the metal lid first.
- *Do* experiment with different ingredients.
- *Do* be creative and have fun making your meals.

- *Don't* put sauces or dressings on top, as they will wilt any lighter vegetables.
- *Don't* leave splashes on the sides of the jar, as the moisture will wilt the lettuce.
- *Don't* put wet ingredients (such as roasted peppers packed in water or oil) on top of the lettuce.
- *Don't* heat or bake mason jars in the oven, as they could break.
- *Don't* be afraid to substitute in other options for ingredients you don't care for or don't have on hand.

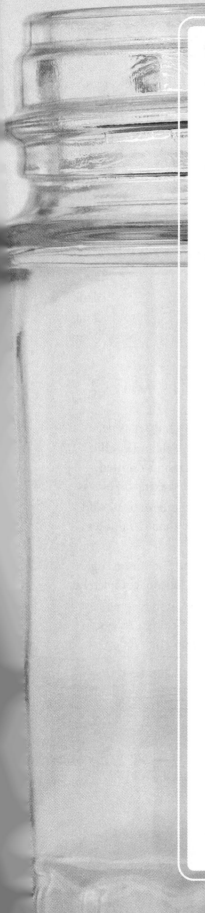

Breakfasts and Snacks

Berry French Toast Bites

If you like French toast, you'll love these little bites, which taste a bit like beignets. The key to keeping them for a few days is not adding any syrup or sauce. I like topping them with fresh raspberries and keeping it simple.

Tip

These bites are pretty sweet as is, but, for each serving, you can pack a 4-oz (125 mL) mason jar with 2 tbsp (30 mL) pure maple syrup for dipping.

- Baking sheet, lined with parchment paper
- Two 8-oz (250 mL) mason jars

3 tbsp	granulated sugar	45 mL
½ tsp	ground cinnamon	2 mL
2	large eggs	2
3 tbsp	milk	45 mL
½ tsp	salt	2 mL
½ tsp	vanilla extract	2 mL
2 cups	cubed stale egg bread (crusts removed)	500 mL
3 tbsp	butter	45 mL
¼ cup	raspberries	60 mL

1. In a large bowl, combine sugar and cinnamon. Set aside.
2. In a large bowl, whisk together eggs, milk, salt and vanilla. Add bread cubes and quickly toss to coat. Using a slotted spoon, lift coated cubes from egg mixture, shaking off excess.
3. In a medium saucepan, melt butter over medium heat. Add coated bread cubes and cook, stirring, for about 2 minutes per side or until browned on all sides.
4. Remove from heat and immediately add to cinnamon sugar, tossing to coat. Spread out on a plate and let cool completely.
5. Place half the bread cubes in each jar. Top with raspberries, dividing evenly. Seal jars and refrigerate for up to 2 days. Serve cold or remove lid and microwave on High for 30 seconds or until warmed through.

Breakfast Burrito in a Jar

This is my take on a breakfast burrito. It doesn't have the wrap, but that doesn't mean you couldn't bring one with you. Or just eat it without. By the time you get to work, it will be at room temperature and ready to eat.

Tip

When chopping avocados to add to a mason jar, squeeze a bit of lemon or lime juice over them to prevent them from browning. In place of the avocado, you could use guacamole with a squeeze of lemon or lime juice.

- Preheat oven to 400°F (200°C)
- Baking sheet, lined with foil
- 1-pint (500 mL) wide-mouth mason jar

1	8-inch (20 cm) flour tortilla	1
2 tbsp	olive oil, divided	30 mL
1	large egg	1
1 tbsp	milk	15 mL
¼ cup	salsa	60 mL
¼ cup	chopped red bell pepper	60 mL
¼ cup	chopped avocado (see tip, at left)	60 mL
¼ cup	diced dry-cured chorizo	60 mL
¼ cup	shredded Cheddar cheese	60 mL

1. Roll flour tortilla into a cylinder and cut into thin strips. In a small bowl, toss tortilla strips with 1 tbsp (15 mL) oil until coated. Arrange strips in a single layer on prepared baking sheet. Bake in preheated oven for 10 minutes or until golden brown. Let cool completely in pan.

2. Meanwhile, in a medium bowl, whisk egg and milk until blended.

3. In a medium skillet, heat the remaining oil over medium heat. Pour in egg mixture, tilting the pan to cover the bottom with a thin layer of egg. Cook for about 3 minutes or until almost set. Turn egg over and cook for 1 minute. Remove from heat and let cool. Once cool, roll egg into a cylinder and cut into thin strips.

4. Add salsa to jar, wiping down any splashes from the side of the jar. Layer egg strips, bell pepper, avocado, chorizo, cheese and tortilla strips on top. Seal jar and refrigerate for up to 2 days. Enjoy straight out of the jar.

Variation

Vegetarian Breakfast Burrito: Replace the chorizo with ¼ cup (60 mL) chopped tomatoes.

Apple Cinnamon Overnight Oatmeal

This is one of those marvel meals. You don't need to cook this oatmeal, just let it sit in the jar overnight. It's amazing and works with just about any flavor combination.

MAKES 1 SERVING

Tip

Leave some room at the top of the jar so the ingredients have room to mix when you shake the jar.

- 1-pint (500 mL) mason jar

½ cup	large-flake (old-fashioned) rolled oats	125 mL
1 tbsp	chopped pecans	15 mL
1 tsp	ground cinnamon	5 mL
¼ cup	milk	60 mL
¼ cup	plain Greek yogurt	60 mL
¼ cup	unsweetened applesauce	60 mL
1 tbsp	liquid honey	15 mL
1 tsp	vanilla extract	5 mL

1. In jar, combine oats, pecans, cinnamon, milk, yogurt, applesauce, honey and vanilla. Stir well, then seal jar and give it a good, vigorous shake to make sure oats are coated with liquid. Refrigerate overnight. Serve cold or remove lid and microwave on High for 1 minute or until warm.

Variation

Substitute ¼ cup (60 mL) chopped apples, tossed in ½ tsp (2 mL) freshly squeezed lemon juice, for the applesauce.

Peanut Butter and Banana Overnight Oatmeal

I feel like I could write a whole book on overnight oatmeal. It's really, really good, and it falls into the category of "Why haven't I done this before?" So here's another to add to your breakfast routine. I encourage you to experiment with your own combinations.

**MAKES
1 SERVING**

Tip

In place of the almond milk, you can use any type of milk you prefer, such as cow's milk or soy milk.

- 1-pint (500 mL) mason jar

½	ripe banana, mashed	½
½ cup	large-flake (old-fashioned) rolled oats	125 mL
1 tsp	ground cinnamon	5 mL
⅓ cup	unsweetened almond milk	75 mL
¼ cup	plain Greek yogurt	60 mL
1 tbsp	peanut butter	15 mL
1 tbsp	liquid honey	15 mL

1. In jar, combine banana, oats, cinnamon, almond milk, yogurt, peanut butter and honey. Stir well, then seal jar and give it a good, vigorous shake to make sure oats are coated with liquid. Refrigerate overnight. Serve cold or remove lid and microwave on High for 1 minute or until warm.

Variation

Chocolate Peanut Butter and Banana Overnight Oatmeal: Substitute chocolate-flavored almond milk for the plain almond milk.

Best Granola Ever

Plain and simple, this is the best granola ever, and it's easy to make, too. Give it a try.

**MAKES
6 SERVINGS**

Tip
Some recipes bake the dried fruit, but it's better to add it just as it comes out of the oven. Baking the fruit can create crunchy, sticky fruit that sticks in your teeth.

- Preheat oven to 300°F (150°C)
- Rimmed baking sheet, lined with parchment paper
- Two 1-quart (1 L) mason jars

3 cups	large-flake (old-fashioned) rolled oats	750 mL
1 cup	coarsely chopped pecans	250 mL
¼ cup	chopped candied ginger	60 mL
1 tsp	ground cinnamon	5 mL
1 tsp	ground ginger	5 mL
¼ tsp	salt	1 mL
3 tbsp	packed brown sugar	45 mL
¼ cup	olive oil	60 mL
⅓ cup	liquid honey	75 mL
¼ cup	dried cherries	60 mL
¼ cup	chopped dried apricots	60 mL
¼ cup	dried cranberries	60 mL

1. In a medium bowl, combine oats, pecans, candied ginger, cinnamon, ground ginger and salt.

2. In a medium saucepan, over medium-low heat, stir brown sugar, oil and honey until smooth. Pour into oat mixture and toss to coat. Spread in an even layer on prepared baking sheet.

3. Bake in preheated oven for about 40 minutes, stirring every 10 minutes, until golden. Stir in cherries, apricots and cranberries, then let cool completely on pan on a wire rack.

4. Divide granola evenly between jars. Seal jars and store at room temperature for up to 1 week.

Variation
Breakfast Yogurt Granola: Add ½ cup (125 mL) granola to an 8-oz (250 mL) mason jar and top with the yogurt of your choice. Seal jar and refrigerate for up to 3 days.

Creamy Fruity Yogurt Cups

I'm not a huge yogurt person, but Greek yogurt changed my breakfast routine. I love how rich and thick it is, and it holds fruit well without becoming too watery.

Tip

You can use any type of yogurt, but full-fat Greek yogurt works best, as it doesn't get thin over time. You don't want the juice from the berries to dilute the yogurt and turn the breakfast into mush.

- 1-pint (500 mL) mason jar

2 tbsp	pure maple syrup	30 mL
½ cup	raspberries	125 mL
½ cup	plain Greek yogurt	125 mL
¼ cup	granola (store-bought or see recipe, opposite)	60 mL

1. Layer maple syrup, raspberries, yogurt and granola in jar. Seal jar and refrigerate for up to 2 days.

Variation

Banana Chocolate Yogurt Cups: Substitute 2 tbsp (30 mL) chocolate syrup for the maple syrup and replace the raspberries with ½ cup (125 mL) sliced bananas.

Triple Berry Ricotta Parfait

Ricotta cheese is a great protein, it spreads on toast, and it is amazingly satisfying with fruit. This is my new go-to breakfast.

Tip

For information on helping your berries last longer, see tip, page 47.

- 1-pint (500 mL) mason jar

½ cup	ricotta cheese	125 mL
¼ cup	blueberries	60 mL
¼ cup	raspberries	60 mL
¼ cup	blackberries	60 mL
1 tbsp	liquid honey	15 mL
2	sprigs fresh mint, chopped	2

1. Spread ricotta evenly in jar. Layer blueberries, raspberries and blackberries on top. Drizzle with honey and top with mint. Seal jar and refrigerate overnight.

Variation

Choco-Berry Ricotta Parfait: Stir 1 tbsp (15 mL) unsweetened cocoa powder into the ricotta before adding it to the jar.

Chocolate Ricotta Strawberry Cups

This breakfast could double as dessert. When serving it as a morning treat, try spreading the ricotta mixture on toast and topping it with the berries. Whatever time of day, it's a perfect treat.

Tip

For a skinny version of this dish, use low-fat ricotta cheese and sugar substitute.

• 8-oz (250 mL) mason jar

1 tbsp	unsweetened cocoa powder	15 mL
1 tsp	granulated sugar	5 mL
½ cup	ricotta cheese	125 mL
1 tbsp	sour cream	15 mL
¼ cup	chopped strawberries	60 mL

1. In a medium bowl, combine cocoa, sugar, ricotta and sour cream until smooth.
2. Spread cheese mixture evenly in jar and top with strawberries. Seal jar and refrigerate for up to 2 days.

"I Need a Little Something" Trail Mix

This snack is the perfect thing to munch on at the office. You can make it in batches and store it in mason jars in your pantry so you always have it on hand when you need a little something. If you want to sub in different nuts or sweets, go for it.

Tip

Resist the urge to use bigger portions. This is a great snack, but it's best to just have a handful of trail mix at a time.

• 8-oz (250 mL) mason jar

¼ cup	unsalted dry-roasted cashews	60 mL
¼ cup	dark chocolate chips	60 mL
¼ cup	dried cranberries	60 mL

1. Layer cashews, chocolate chips and cranberries in jar. Seal jar and store at room temperature for up to 1 week. Shake before serving.

Variation

Candied Pecan and Dried Cranberries: Omit the cashews and chocolate chips and use ½ cup (125 mL) candied pecans.

Chocolate Protein Smoothie

I've never been a protein drink kind of girl, but if you are on the go and finding time for breakfast is proving to be a challenge, this smoothie is an easy alternative.

Tip

If you can't find chocolate-flavored protein powder, use plain protein powder and add 1 tsp (5 mL) unsweetened cocoa powder.

- Blender
- 1-pint (500 mL) mason jar

10	ice cubes	10
1	banana	1
1 cup	chocolate-flavored almond milk	250 mL
½ tsp	vanilla extract	2 mL
¼ cup	chocolate-flavored protein powder	60 mL
¼ cup	plain Greek yogurt	60 mL

1. In blender, combine ice cubes, banana, almond milk, vanilla, protein powder and yogurt; blend until smooth.
2. Pour smoothie into jar and serve immediately or seal jar and refrigerate for up to 1 day. If the smoothie separates, shake jar vigorously until smooth.

Variation

Chocolate Orange Smoothie: Replace the banana with 1 peeled orange.

Peanut Butter and Jam Smoothie

My husband is a smoothie lover. He makes one every morning. And as he's blending at full speed, ice crunching at an irritating decibel, he screams Katy Perry songs to override the noise. I pretend it annoys me, but I can't help smiling when that blender revs up. Our boys sing along too. This is an easy breakfast, riffing on the classic sandwich.

Tips

Smoothies are best when made the morning of. They will last the day, but you'll need to shake them up before drinking.

If you use fresh strawberries, you may need to add 1 or 2 more ice cubes to get the desired consistency.

- Blender
- Two 8-oz (250 mL) mason jars

10	ice cubes	10
1 cup	frozen or fresh strawberries	250 mL
1 cup	unsweetened almond milk	250 mL
¼ cup	plain Greek yogurt	60 mL
1 tbsp	peanut butter	15 mL
1 tsp	liquid honey	5 mL

1. In blender, combine ice cubes, strawberries, almond milk, yogurt, peanut butter and honey; blend until smooth.
2. Divide smoothie evenly between jars and serve immediately or seal jars and refrigerate for up to 1 day. If the smoothie separates, shake jar vigorously until smooth.

Variation

If you don't have any strawberries on hand, omit the honey and add 2 tbsp (30 mL) jam of your choice.

Peanut Butter, Honey and Apples

I know what you are thinking: you don't need a recipe for peanut butter and honey. That's true, but you do need inspiration for healthy snacks to bring to work. This combination never disappoints.

Tip

You can use any firm fruit, such as sliced pears. Just make sure, if you are making it the night before, to squeeze lemon juice over the fruit to prevent it from browning.

- Two 4-oz (125 mL) mason jars

¼ cup	peanut butter	60 mL
1 tbsp	liquid honey	15 mL
1	apple, sliced	1
1 tsp	lemon juice	5 mL
1 tsp	fresh thyme leaves	5 mL

1. Layer peanut butter and honey in one jar. Place apple slices in the other jar, sprinkle with lemon juice and top with thyme. Seal jars and refrigerate for up to 1 day.

2. To serve, dip the apple slices in the peanut butter mixture.

Variation

Peanut Butter with Apples and Cinnamon: In place of the lemon juice, add 1 tsp (5 mL) ground cinnamon to the apples and toss to coat thoroughly. The cinnamon hides the browning on the apples but also makes this snack so delicious.

Hummus Snack Pack

There's nothing new about having hummus as a snack, but making it from scratch is unbelievably easy. Make a larger batch and store individual containers in the refrigerator.

Tip

Pack cherry tomatoes and crackers in sealable plastic bags to dip in your hummus.

- Food processor
- Three 4-oz (125 mL) mason jars

1	can (14 to 19 oz/398 to 540 mL) chickpeas, drained and rinsed	1
1	clove garlic, minced	1
3 tbsp	water	45 mL
2 tbsp	extra virgin olive oil	30 mL
1 tsp	fresh thyme leaves	5 mL
	Salt and freshly ground black pepper	

1. In food processor, combine chickpeas, garlic, water and $1\frac{1}{2}$ tbsp (22 mL) oil; purée until smooth.
2. Divide purée among jars and sprinkle with thyme, salt and pepper to taste, and the remaining oil. Seal jar and refrigerate for up to 3 days.

Variations

Creamy Hummus: For a velvety texture, add 1 tbsp (15 mL) tahini to the purée.

Spicy Hummus: Add 1 tbsp (15 mL) hot pepper sauce to the purée.

Seven-Layer Dip

If there were ever a recipe to go into a mason jar, this would be it. The layers make it a food stylist's dream. With the contrasting colors of the guacamole, salsa and cheese, it's beautiful to look at and a joy to eat. And, I might add, it is the perfect potluck snack to bring to work.

**MAKES
4 SERVINGS**

Tips

If you can, use a wide-mouth mason jar for the dip. Otherwise, you'll have to scoop it onto a plate with a long-handled spoon as needed.

This dip doesn't have to be seven layers: you could make it eight or nine layers instead. Add chopped iceberg lettuce, chopped red bell peppers or chopped drained artichokes before the cilantro.

- 1-quart (1 L) wide-mouth mason jar
- 8-oz (250 mL) mason jar

1 cup	refried beans	250 mL
1 tbsp	taco seasoning	15 mL
2	ripe avocados	2
1 tbsp	freshly squeezed lime juice	15 mL
1 cup	sour cream	250 mL
1 cup	salsa	250 mL
1 cup	shredded Cheddar cheese	250 mL
½ cup	sliced black or green olives	125 mL
½ cup	chopped seeded tomatoes	125 mL
¼ cup	chopped seeded jalapeño peppers	60 mL
¼ cup	roughly chopped fresh cilantro	60 mL
2 cups	tortilla chips	500 mL

1. In a small bowl, combine refried beans and taco seasoning.
2. In another bowl, mash avocados with lime juice.
3. Layer bean mixture, sour cream, avocado mixture, salsa, cheese, olives, tomatoes, jalapeños and cilantro in the 1-quart (1 L) mason jar. Seal jar and refrigerate for up to 3 days.
4. Place tortillas in the 8-oz (250 mL) jar. Seal jar and store in a dry area until ready to serve with the dip.

Variation

Skinny Seven-Layer Dip: Replace the sour cream with nonfat Greek yogurt, use shredded part-skim mozzarella cheese in place of the Cheddar and pack baked tortilla chips instead of fried.

Soups

Chilled Mango Soup

Fruit soups can be dessert, a first course during dinner or a refreshing complement to a light lunch. You can make this soup a few days before you plan to serve it.

Tip

This is an ideal make-ahead soup, as the flavors get better the longer it is chilled.

- Blender or food processor
- Four 1-pint (500 mL) mason jars

2	mangos, chopped	2
1	English cucumber, diced, divided	1
1 cup	cold water	250 mL
2 tbsp	freshly squeezed lime juice	30 mL
	Salt and freshly ground black pepper	
½ cup	sliced red bell pepper	125 mL
1 cup	sliced red onion	250 mL
1 cup	chopped fresh mint	250 mL
1 tbsp	chopped seeded jalapeño pepper	15 mL

1. In blender, combine mangos, half the cucumber and cold water; purée until almost smooth. Stir in lime juice and season to taste with salt and pepper.

2. Divide the remaining cucumber evenly among jars. Layer red pepper and onion on top. Pour in mango purée, dividing evenly. Top with mint and jalapeño. Seal jars and refrigerate for at least 4 hours, until chilled, or for up to 3 days. Stir before serving.

Variation

Chilled Mango and Shrimp Soup: When serving the soup, top each serving with 3 cold cooked shrimp.

Chilled Celery Soup

This simple and inexpensive soup is absolutely delicious. Enjoy it all summer long and serve it right out of the jars. It's a great first course to enjoy during a backyard barbecue.

MAKES 4 SERVINGS	

Tip

For added flavor, save the celery fronds and finely chop them to use as a garnish.

- Immersion blender or food processor
- Four 1-pint (500 mL) mason jars

2 tbsp	olive oil	30 mL
1 tbsp	unsalted butter	15 mL
1 cup	diced peeled potato	250 mL
1 cup	finely chopped onion	250 mL
1	head celery, trimmed, stalks chopped	1
4 cups	ready-to-use chicken or vegetable broth	1 L
	Salt and freshly ground black pepper	
½ cup	chopped fresh cilantro	125 mL
¼ cup	chopped fresh parsley	60 mL
½ cup	table (18%) cream	125 mL

1. In a large pot, heat oil and butter over medium heat until butter foams. Stir in potato and onion; reduce heat to low and cook, stirring, until potato is tender and onion is golden. Transfer half of the potato mixture to a bowl and set aside.

2. Add celery and broth to the pot; bring to a boil over high heat. Reduce heat and simmer for 10 minutes. Using an immersion blender (or transferring soup in batches to a food processor), purée soup until smooth. Season to taste with salt and pepper. Let cool completely.

3. Divide reserved potato mixture evenly among jars. Top with cilantro, then carefully pour in soup, dividing evenly. Sprinkle with parsley and drizzle with cream. Seal jars and refrigerate for at least 4 hours, until chilled, or for up to 2 days. Stir before serving.

Variation

Chilled Celery and Prosciutto Soup: Arrange 4 prosciutto slices on a foil-lined baking sheet and bake in a 450°F (230°C) oven for 10 minutes or until crispy. Let cool completely, then chop. Sprinkle on top with the parsley.

End of Summer Spanish Cold Soup

There is no such thing as basic gazpacho, as this version proves.

**MAKES
4 SERVINGS**

Tips

If you don't have any baguette on hand but have bread crumbs in the pantry, soften ¼ cup (60 mL) with water and gradually add them to the food processor before the oil.

If you can't find Spanish ham, you can substitute ½ cup (125 mL) chopped prosciutto.

• Food processor
• Four 1-pint (500 mL) mason jars

1	3-inch (7.5 cm) piece of baguette, cut into cubes	1
¼ cup	water	60 mL
3	hard-cooked eggs, yolks and whites separated and whites chopped	3
2	cloves garlic, crushed	2
½ tsp	salt	2 mL
3 tbsp	sherry vinegar	45 mL
½ cup	mild virgin olive oil	125 mL
2 lbs	ripe tomatoes, chopped (including juices)	1 kg
1 cup	chopped Spanish ham	250 mL
1 cup	finely chopped green bell pepper	250 mL

1. In a bowl, soak baguette cubes in water for 1 minute. Squeeze bread dry and discard soaking water.

2. In food processor, combine soaked bread, egg yolks, garlic, salt and vinegar; process until smooth. With the motor running, through the feed tube, add oil in a slow stream and process until a thick sauce forms.

3. Divide sauce evenly among jars. Layer tomatoes, ham, green pepper and egg whites on top. Seal jars and refrigerate for at least 4 hours, until chilled, or for up to 2 days. Stir before serving.

Variation

Spanish Cold Soup with Shrimp: When serving the soup, top each serving with 3 cold poached shrimp.

Middle Eastern Yogurt Soup

Fans of cold soup will adore this version of the traditional cucumber and yogurt cooler. The secret ingredient, golden raisins, gives it an extraordinary flavor boost.

Tips

To toast walnut halves, spread them in a dry skillet over medium-high heat and cook, stirring often, for 1 to 2 minutes or until golden brown. Let cool completely, then chop.

If you want to thin out your soup, add 2 ice cubes to each jar and let them thin it as they melt.

- Four to six 1-pint (500 mL) mason jars

1 cup	golden raisins	250 mL
1 cup	finely chopped fresh dill, divided	250 mL
½ cup	finely chopped fresh mint	125 mL
4 cups	plain Greek yogurt	1 L
1 cup	ice water	250 mL
1	English cucumber, finely chopped	1
1 cup	toasted walnut halves (see tip, at left), finely chopped	250 mL

1. In a large bowl, combine raisins, all but 1 tbsp (15 mL) dill, mint, yogurt and ice water.
2. Divide cucumbers evenly among jars. Layer walnuts, yogurt mixture and the remaining dill on top. Seal jars and refrigerate for at least 4 hours, until chilled, or for up to 3 days. Stir before serving.

Variation

Smoked Salmon and Yogurt Soup: When serving the soup, top each serving with 1 tbsp (15 mL) chopped smoked salmon.

Avocado and Crab Soup

This is one of those cold soups that tastes way better than it looks. Its color, as my son Murray says, is "monster green." But don't let that scare you. The taste is awesome.

Tip

I discovered this tip while googling one day. It's credited to Erica, a food blogger at *Northwest Edible Life*. When I read it, I had one of those aha moments. If you are trying to figure out whether an avocado is ripe, pluck off the stem. If the stem is brown, so is your avocado. If it's healthy-looking and green, the same goes for the creamy fruit.

- Blender
- 1-quart (1 L) mason jar

¼ cup	fresh or drained thawed frozen backfin (lump) crabmeat	60 mL
1 tsp	chopped fresh cilantro	5 mL
1 tbsp	freshly squeezed lime juice	15 mL
1	avocado, flesh scooped out	1
½ tsp	salt	2 mL
½ tsp	freshly ground black pepper	2 mL
1 cup	ready-to-use chicken broth	250 mL
1 cup	water	250 mL
2 tbsp	crème fraîche	30 mL

1. In a small bowl, combine crab, cilantro and lime juice.
2. In blender, combine avocado, salt, pepper, broth, water and crème fraîche; blend on high until well combined.
3. Pour avocado soup into jar and top with crab mixture. Seal jar and refrigerate for at least 4 hours, until chilled, or for up to 3 days. Stir before serving.

Variation

Lobster and Avocado Soup: Substitute chopped thawed frozen lobster meat for the crab.

Squash Soup with Yogurt and Chives

This seems like a winter soup, but it can — and should — be enjoyed any time of year.

Tips

Butternut squash is delicious but is a bland vegetable. It's important to use flavorful chicken broth and to season the soup well.

Use caution when removing the jar from the microwave, as the soup could be quite hot.

- 1-pint (500 mL) mason jar

1 tbsp	olive oil	15 mL
¼ cup	finely chopped onion	60 mL
1 tsp	finely chopped garlic	5 mL
1 tsp	curry powder	5 mL
1 cup	thawed frozen butternut squash purée	250 mL
1 tsp	chopped fresh thyme	5 mL
½ cup	ready-to-use chicken broth	125 mL
3 tbsp	plain Greek yogurt	45 mL
	Salt and freshly ground black pepper	
2 tbsp	chopped fresh chives	30 mL

1. In a medium saucepan, heat oil over medium-high heat. Add onion, garlic and curry powder; cook, stirring, for 3 minutes or until onion is softened. Stir in squash, thyme and broth. Whisk in yogurt. Season to taste with salt and pepper.
2. Pour soup into jar and sprinkle with chives. Seal jar and refrigerate for up to 3 days.
3. When ready to serve, remove lid and microwave on High for 3 to 4 minutes, stopping to stir after 2 minutes, until heated through. Stir again before serving.

Variation

Bacon Squash Soup: Serve the soup garnished with ¼ cup (60 mL) chopped cooked bacon.

Chickpea Minestrone

For all of you who think mason jar lunches are lighter fare, I dare you to try this soup. It's so simple, yet it fills me up for the afternoon. A piece of crusty bread is all you need to accompany it.

Tips

A spoonful of pesto is a good way to add instant flavor to a soup. Traditional basil pesto works with most soups, but you can also try alternatives such as sun-dried tomato pesto or arugula pesto.

Use caution when removing the jar from the microwave, as the soup could be quite hot.

- 1-quart (1 L) mason jar

1 tbsp	olive oil	15 mL
¼ cup	finely chopped onion	60 mL
¼ cup	finely chopped celery	60 mL
¼ cup	finely chopped carrots	60 mL
1 tsp	chopped fresh thyme	5 mL
	Salt and freshly ground black pepper	
½ cup	finely chopped tomatoes	125 mL
¼ cup	peas	60 mL
½ cup	rinsed drained canned chickpeas	125 mL
1½ cups	ready-to-use chicken broth	375 mL
1 tbsp	finely chopped fresh parsley	15 mL
1 tbsp	pesto	15 mL

1. In a medium skillet, heat oil over medium-high heat. Add onion, celery, carrots and thyme; cook, stirring, for 5 minutes or until vegetables are softened. Season to taste with salt and pepper. Let cool completely.

2. Layer onion mixture, tomatoes, peas and chickpeas in jar. Pour in broth and top with parsley. Dollop pesto on top. Seal jar and refrigerate for up to 3 days.

3. When ready to serve, remove lid and microwave on High for 3 to 4 minutes, stopping to stir after 2 minutes, until heated through. Stir again before serving.

Variation

Traditional Minestrone: Add 1 cup (250 mL) cooled cooked small or baby shell pasta and 2 tbsp (30 mL) freshly grated Parmesan cheese. Layer in this order: onion mixture, peas, chickpeas, tomatoes, pasta, broth, parsley, pesto and cheese.

Tex-Mex Black Bean Soup

This is one of those hearty soups that I could eat every day. It's filling, it has a bit of kick, and it is loaded with fiber and vegetables.

SOUPS 33

**MAKES
1 SERVING**

Tips

Just before serving, add a dollop of sour cream to the soup to add creaminess.

Use caution when removing the jar from the microwave, as the soup could be quite hot.

- 1-quart (1 L) mason jar
- 4-oz (125 mL) mason jar

1 tbsp	olive oil	15 mL
½ cup	finely chopped onion	125 mL
½ cup	finely chopped green bell pepper	125 mL
	Salt and freshly ground black pepper	
1 tbsp	chopped chipotle pepper in adobo sauce	15 mL
1 cup	rinsed drained canned black beans	250 mL
½ cup	chopped tomatoes	125 mL
½ cup	frozen corn kernels	125 mL
1½ cups	ready-to-use chicken broth	375 mL
½ cup	chopped avocado	125 mL
1 tbsp	chopped fresh cilantro	15 mL
1 tsp	freshly squeezed lemon juice	5 mL

1. In a medium skillet, heat oil over medium-high heat. Add onion, green pepper and salt and pepper to taste; cook, stirring, for 5 minutes or until vegetables are softened. Add chipotle and cook, stirring, for 1 minute. Let cool completely.

2. Layer onion mixture, beans, tomatoes and corn in the 1-quart (1 L) jar. Pour in broth. Seal jar and refrigerate for up to 3 days.

3. In the 4-oz (125 mL) jar, combine avocado, cilantro and lemon juice. Seal jar and refrigerate for up to 2 days.

4. When ready to serve, remove lid from soup and microwave on High for 3 to 4 minutes, stopping to stir after 2 minutes, until heated through. Stir again, then serve topped with avocado mixture.

Variation

Chicken Black Bean Soup: When serving the soup, top it with ½ cup (125 mL) shredded cooked chicken. Heat it up for 1 minute in the microwave first, if desired.

Edamame Succotash Soup

Whenever we take a trip to Florida, my husband, Mike, rediscovers succotash and reminds me of how much he loves it. This soup is for him, only I added edamame for a twist.

Tips

If you don't have time to let the edamame thaw, just throw them in boiling water for 2 to 3 minutes. Drain and they are good to go.

Use caution when removing the jar from the microwave, as the soup could be quite hot.

- 1-quart (1 L) mason jar

1 tbsp	olive oil	15 mL
¼ cup	chopped bacon	60 mL
¼ cup	finely chopped onion	60 mL
1 tsp	finely chopped garlic	5 mL
	Salt and freshly ground black pepper	
½ cup	diced tomatoes	125 mL
¼ cup	frozen corn kernels	60 mL
¼ cup	chopped red bell pepper	60 mL
¼ cup	thawed frozen edamame	60 mL
1½ cups	ready-to-use chicken broth	375 mL
1 tbsp	chopped fresh basil	15 mL

1. In a medium skillet, heat oil over medium-high heat. Add bacon, onion and garlic; cook, stirring, for 5 to 7 minutes or until bacon is crisp and onion is browned. Drain off fat and season to taste with salt and pepper. Let cool completely.

2. Layer bacon mixture, tomatoes, corn, red pepper and edamame in jar. Pour in broth and top with basil. Seal jar and refrigerate for up to 3 days.

3. When ready to serve, remove lid and microwave on High for 3 to 4 minutes, stopping to stir after 2 minutes, until heated through. Stir again before serving.

Variation

Chicken Succotash Soup: Add ¼ cup (60 mL) cold shredded cooked chicken after the basil.

Bok Choy, Tofu and Shiitake Soup

You can use any mushrooms you like in this light and flavorful soup, but shiitake mushrooms really shine. The preparation is easy, so double the recipe and have this soup on hand for when you want a snack.

Tips

To clean mushrooms, fill a bowl with water, add the mushrooms and swirl them around. Drain and pat dry with a towel. Alternatively, you can simply use a brush to scrape the dirt off.

Use caution when removing the jar from the microwave, as the soup could be quite hot.

● **1-quart (1 L) mason jar**

1 tbsp	olive oil	15 mL
¼ cup	finely chopped onion	60 mL
1 tsp	finely chopped garlic	5 mL
½ cup	sliced shiitake mushroom caps	125 mL
1 cup	chopped bok choy	250 mL
¼ cup	diced firm tofu	60 mL
1½ cups	ready-to-use vegetable broth	375 mL
1 tsp	fish sauce (nam pla)	5 mL
1 tsp	soy sauce	5 mL
¼ tsp	hot pepper sauce	1 mL

1. In a medium skillet, heat oil over medium-high heat. Add onion and garlic; cook, stirring, for 3 minutes or until softened. Let cool completely.

2. Layer onion mixture, mushrooms, bok choy and tofu in jar. Pour in broth, fish sauce, soy sauce and hot pepper sauce. Seal jar and refrigerate for up to 3 days.

3. When ready to serve, remove lid and microwave on High for 3 to 4 minutes, stopping to stir after 2 minutes, until heated through. Stir again before serving.

Variation

Chicken, Bok Choy and Shiitake Soup: When serving the soup, top it with ¼ cup (60 mL) shredded cooked chicken. Heat it up for 1 minute in the microwave first, if desired.

Asian Vegetable and Tofu Soup

This soup is a fresh take on a traditional soup in a cup. Bring the jar to work and just add boiling water. I like using snap peas and bean sprouts, but any crunchy vegetables will do.

**MAKES
1 SERVING**

Tips

To "julienne" means to cut into matchstick-shaped pieces. For the carrots in this recipe, trim off the rounded ends of each piece, then cut into ⅛-inch (3 mm) thick strips. Cut the snap peas on the diagonal into ⅛-inch (3 mm) thick strips.

It's best to pack this soup tightly. If the jar isn't fully stuffed, the vegetables will settle after a day or two in the refrigerator. With the back of a spoon, press the vegetables down to compact them, leaving just a little room at the top. The tofu should rest right at the top of the jar.

- **1-quart (1 L) mason jar**

1 tbsp	powdered chicken bouillon	15 mL
1 tsp	hoisin sauce	5 mL
¼ tsp	hot pepper sauce	1 mL
½ cup	julienned carrots (see tip, at left)	125 mL
1½ cups	chopped napa cabbage	375 mL
1 cup	bean sprouts	250 mL
½ cup	julienned snap peas	125 mL
¼ cup	chopped green onions	60 mL
1 tbsp	sliced gingerroot	15 mL
⅓ cup	cubed firm tofu (½-inch/1 cm cubes)	75 mL
½ tsp	sesame oil	2 mL
1½ cups	boiling water	375 mL

1. Add bouillon, hoisin and hot pepper sauce to the jar, coating the bottom. Layer carrots, cabbage, bean sprouts, peas, green onions, ginger, tofu and sesame oil on top. Seal jar and refrigerate for up to 2 days.

2. When ready to serve, stir in boiling water and let stand for 2 minutes before serving.

Variation

Asian Chicken Soup: Substitute ⅓ cup (75 mL) chopped grilled chicken for the tofu.

Super-Quick Shrimp and Corn Soup

This is a simple and tasty soup to make and take for lunch. Just throw all the ingredients into a mason jar and heat it up before eating — that's it!

Tips

To "julienne" means to cut into matchstick-shaped pieces. For this recipe, cut the snap peas on the diagonal into $1/8$-inch (3 mm) thick strips.

This is a versatile soup. Any vegetable that you like that can be enjoyed raw or slightly cooked will work well.

Use caution when removing the jar from the microwave, as the soup could be quite hot.

- 1-quart (1 L) mason jar

¼ cup	frozen corn kernels	60 mL
¼ cup	finely chopped red bell pepper	60 mL
¼ cup	julienned snap peas (see tip, at left)	60 mL
½ cup	chopped bok choy	125 mL
¼ cup	thawed frozen medium cooked shrimp	60 mL
1½ cups	ready-to-use chicken broth	375 mL
1 tsp	sesame oil	5 mL
½ tsp	soy sauce	2 mL
½ tsp	hot pepper sauce	2 mL

1. Layer corn, red pepper, peas, bok choy and shrimp in jar. Pour in broth, oil, soy sauce and hot pepper sauce. Seal jar and refrigerate for up to 3 days.

2. When ready to serve, remove lid and microwave on High for 3 to 4 minutes, stopping to stir after 2 minutes, until heated through. Stir again before serving.

Variation

Shrimp, Chicken and Corn Soup: When serving the soup, top it with ¼ cup (60 mL) shredded cooked chicken. Heat it up for 1 minute in the microwave first, if desired.

Chicken Soup in a Jar

This is a dumbed-down version of chicken soup. All the pieces are there, you just cheat the cooking for hours and use store-bought chicken broth.

Tips

To make this even easier, buy a rotisserie chicken, pull it apart with a fork and measure 1 cup (250 mL). Use the remaining shredded chicken in other recipes.

Use caution when removing the jar from the microwave, as the soup could be quite hot.

- 1-quart (1 L) mason jar

6 cups	water, divided	1.5 L
4 oz	boneless skinless chicken breast	125 g
	Salt	
1 cup	egg noodles	250 mL
1 tbsp	olive oil	15 mL
1 cup	finely chopped carrots	250 mL
1 cup	finely chopped celery	250 mL
½ cup	finely chopped white onion	125 mL
2 tbsp	chopped fresh thyme	30 mL
	Freshly ground black pepper	
1½ cups	ready-to-use chicken broth	375 mL
¼ cup	chopped fresh parsley	60 mL

1. In a medium saucepan, bring 3 cups (750 mL) water to a boil over medium-high heat. Add chicken, reduce heat and simmer for 15 minutes or until no longer pink inside. Let stand in water for 5 minutes. Drain, transfer chicken to a plate and let cool completely, then pull meat apart with a fork.

2. Meanwhile, in another medium saucepan, bring 3 cups (750 mL) salted water to a boil over high heat. Add noodles and boil for 5 minutes or until firm to the bite. Drain noodles and let cool completely.

3. Meanwhile, in a medium skillet, heat oil over medium-high heat. Add carrots, celery and onion; cook, stirring, for 5 minutes or until softened. Stir in thyme and season to taste with pepper.

4. Layer carrot mixture, noodles and chicken in jar. Pour in broth and top with parsley. Seal jar and refrigerate for up to 3 days.

5. When ready to serve, remove lid and microwave on High for 3 to 4 minutes, stopping to stir after 2 minutes, until heated through. Stir again before serving.

Variation

Mock Chicken Soup: Replace the chicken broth with ready-to-use vegetable broth and substitute 1 cup (250 mL) cubed firm tofu for the chicken.

Pizza Soup

When I was growing up, my mother used to make pizza fondue for my sister and me. It consisted of hot tomato sauce with pepperoni and melted mozzarella cheese. I thought it would translate into an easy mason-jar lunch. Serve with a few pieces of crusty baguette.

Tip

Use caution when removing the jar from the microwave, as the soup could be quite hot.

- 1-quart (1 L) mason jar
- 4-oz (125 mL) mason jar

1 tbsp	olive oil	15 mL
¼ cup	finely chopped onion	60 mL
1 tsp	finely chopped garlic	5 mL
	Salt and freshly ground black pepper	
1 cup	canned crushed tomatoes	250 mL
1 tsp	dried oregano	5 mL
¼ cup	chopped pepperoni	60 mL
1 cup	ready-to-use chicken broth	250 mL
¼ cup	shredded mozzarella cheese	60 mL

1. In a medium skillet, heat oil over medium-high heat. Add onion and garlic; cook, stirring, for 3 minutes or until softened. Season to taste with salt and pepper. Let cool completely.

2. Layer onion mixture, tomatoes, oregano and pepperoni in the 1-quart (1 L) jar. Pour in broth. Seal jar and refrigerate for up to 3 days.

3. Place cheese in the 4-oz (125 mL) jar. Seal jar and refrigerate for up to 3 days.

4. When ready to serve, remove lids and add cheese to soup. Microwave soup on High for 3 to 4 minutes, stopping to stir after 2 minutes, until heated through. Stir again before serving.

Black Bean and Chorizo Soup

The chorizo sausage gives this robust soup a kick. Buy either mild or spicy chorizo, to get the heat you want.

**MAKES
4 SERVINGS**

Tips

Keep an eye on the soup while reheating it in the microwave, as it may splatter. And use caution when removing the jar from the microwave, as the soup could be quite hot.

If reheating more than one jar at once, double the time in the microwave, stopping occasionally to stir.

Variation

Black Bean, Chorizo and Chicken Soup:
Add ½ cup (125 mL) cold shredded cooked chicken to each jar before adding the sour cream.

- Immersion blender or food processor
- Four 1-pint (500 mL) mason jars

1 tbsp	olive oil	15 mL
2	smoked chorizo sausages, roughly chopped	2
½ cup	chopped red onion	125 mL
1 tbsp	chopped garlic	15 mL
1½ tsp	ground cumin	7 mL
1 tsp	dried oregano	5 mL
1	bay leaf	1
1 cup	rinsed drained canned black beans	250 mL
4 cups	ready-to-use chicken or vegetable broth	1 L
½ cup	chopped fresh cilantro	125 mL
½ cup	sour cream	125 mL

1. In a large, heavy saucepan, heat oil over medium heat. Add chorizo and cook, stirring, until browned. Using a slotted spoon, transfer sausage to a plate lined with paper towels and set aside.

2. Add onion and garlic to the pan and cook, stirring, for about 5 minutes or until softened. Add cumin and oregano; cook, stirring, for 1 minute.

3. Stir in bay leaf, beans and broth; bring to a boil. Reduce heat and simmer for 30 minutes. Using an immersion blender (or transferring soup in batches to a food processor), purée soup until smooth. Let cool completely.

4. Divide chorizo evenly among jars and sprinkle with cilantro. Gently pour in soup and top with sour cream. Seal jars and refrigerate for up to 2 days.

5. Serve cold or remove the lid and microwave on High for 3 to 4 minutes, stopping to stir after 2 minutes, until heated through. Stir again before serving.

White Bean, Sausage and Kale Soup

This soup is hearty, satisfying and comforting. You could substitute kidney beans or chickpeas for the white beans; the result is just as good.

Tips

Make sure to thoroughly rinse the beans under cold water. If you don't, your soup will have a thick, goopy texture.

Use caution when removing the jar from the microwave, as the soup could be quite hot.

- Preheat broiler
- Baking sheet, lined with foil
- 1-quart (1 L) mason jar

1	Italian sausage	1
1 tbsp	olive oil	15 mL
¼ cup	finely chopped onion	60 mL
1 tsp	finely chopped garlic	5 mL
	Salt and freshly ground black pepper	
½ cup	rinsed drained canned white beans	125 mL
1 cup	chopped trimmed kale	250 mL
1½ cups	ready-to-use chicken broth	375 mL

1. Place sausage on prepared baking sheet and pierce all over with a fork. Broil on the top rack of the oven for 10 to 12 minutes, turning once, until juices run clear. Let cool, then cut into circles.

2. Meanwhile, in a medium skillet, heat oil over medium-high heat. Add onion and garlic; cook, stirring, for 3 minutes or until softened. Season to taste with salt and pepper. Let cool completely.

3. Layer onion mixture, beans, kale and sausage in jar. Pour in broth. Seal jar and refrigerate for up to 3 days.

4. When ready to serve, remove lid and microwave on High for 3 to 4 minutes, stopping to stir after 2 minutes, until heated through. Stir again before serving.

Variation

Pasta, Sausage and Kale Soup: Replace the white beans with ½ cup (125 mL) cooled cooked orecchiette.

Fruit and Vegetable Salads

Waldorf Salad

Named after the Waldorf Hotel in New York City, where it was first created, this salad is an American classic. Raisins are a traditional ingredient, but if you are squeamish about them, as I am, just leave them out.

Tip

Granny Smith is my apple of choice here, but any crisp apple, such as Gala or Honey Crisp, will work as well.

- Preheat oven to 350°F (180°C)
- 1-quart (1 L) mason jar

¼ cup	walnut halves	60 mL
2 tbsp	mayonnaise	30 mL
2 tsp	freshly squeezed lemon juice	10 mL
	Salt and freshly ground black pepper	
1 cup	chopped celery, including leaves	250 mL
¼ cup	chopped fresh flat-leaf (Italian) parsley	60 mL
1 cup	cubed Granny Smith apple	250 mL
¼ cup	raisins	60 mL
1½ cups	Boston lettuce	375 mL

1. Spread walnuts in a single layer on a baking sheet. Bake in preheated oven for 5 to 10 minutes or until golden brown. Check often, as they can burn quickly. Let cool completely.

2. In a small bowl, whisk together mayonnaise and lemon juice. Season to taste with salt and pepper.

3. Spoon dressing into jar, wiping down any splashes on the side of the jar. Layer celery, parsley, apples, raisins, lettuce and walnuts on top. Seal jar and refrigerate for up to 3 days.

4. When ready to serve, turn jar upside down in a bowl and let dressing coat the salad.

Variation

Chicken Waldorf Salad: Add ½ cup (125 mL) cold cubed cooked chicken before the walnuts.

Apple, Pancetta and Frisée Salad

I created this salad years ago, and it has become my go-to at dinnertime. After nibbling on it one night, I realized the apple rounds and pancetta slices are perfectly suited for a mason jar. Voilà! Here's the portable version of my dinner salad staple.

**MAKES
1 SERVING**

Tips

Make sure to leave enough space for the pancetta. Do not pack the pancetta in tightly or it will get soggy.

You can replace the frisée with watercress, arugula or any firmer leaf lettuce.

- Preheat oven to 450°F (230°C)
- Rimmed baking sheet, lined with foil
- 1-quart (1 L) mason jar

4	slices pancetta	4
1 cup	thinly sliced Granny Smith apple	250 mL
	Juice of 1 lemon, divided	
2 tbsp	extra virgin olive oil	30 mL
1 cup	sliced cucumber	250 mL
	(¼-inch/0.5 cm rounds)	
2 cups	packed frisée	500 mL
½ cup	crumbled feta cheese	125 mL
	Freshly ground black pepper	

1. Arrange pancetta on prepared baking sheet. Bake in preheated oven for 10 minutes or until crispy. Let cool completely.
2. Place apples in a medium bowl and drizzle with half the lemon juice, tossing to coat.
3. Pour oil and the remaining lemon juice into jar, wiping down any splashes on the side of the jar.
4. Drain apples and discard excess juice. Layer cucumber, apple, frisée and feta on top of oil mixture. Place pancetta gently on top. Seal jar and refrigerate for up to 3 days.
5. When ready to serve, turn jar upside down in a bowl and let dressing coat the salad. Season to taste with pepper.

Pear, Pomegranate and Asiago Salad

This salad is simple and refreshing. It makes for an elegant lunch — or supersize it and prepare it in a serving bowl to serve as a side at a dinner party.

Tips

The best way to seed a pomegranate is to cut it in half crosswise, stretch each half to loosen the seeds and whack the back of the fruit with a wooden spoon. All the seeds should fall out in seconds.

You can replace the Asiago with any cheese you like, such as shaved Parmesan or crumbled goat cheese or blue cheese.

- 1-quart (1 L) mason jar

1 cup	sliced pears	250 mL
	Juice of ½ lemon	
2 tbsp	Citrus Vinaigrette (page 166)	30 mL
¼ cup	pomegranate seeds	60 mL
2 cups	packed frisée	500 mL
¼ cup	shaved Asiago cheese	60 mL
¼ cup	candied pecans	60 mL

1. Add pears and lemon juice to a medium bowl of water and let stand for 5 minutes. Drain and pat dry.
2. Pour vinaigrette into jar, wiping down any splashes on the side of the jar. Layer pears, pomegranate seeds, frisée, cheese and pecans on top. Seal jar and refrigerate for up to 3 days.
3. When ready to serve, turn jar upside down in a bowl and let the dressing coat the salad.

Triple Berry Spinach Salad

This is my version of a strawberry spinach salad. I packed in three types of berries for more interest, but if you are a traditional spinach salad eater, strawberries on their own are just as delicious.

Tips

To keep your berries fresh and help them last longer, prewash them in a vinegar-water mixture. Combine 3 cups (750 mL) water with 1 cup (125 mL) white vinegar and gently wash the berries. Lay them on a paper towel to dry or use a salad spinner to remove excess moisture. Store in a bowl lined with paper towels or a plastic container with the lid not tightly sealed, to release moisture.

Be sure to loosely pack the spinach in this salad, as the fruits are fragile.

You can substitute goat cheese for the blue cheese, if you prefer.

The walnuts can be replaced with candied pecans.

* **1-quart (1 L) mason jar**

2 tbsp	Lemon Poppy Seed Vinaigrette (page 165)	30 mL
½ cup	blueberries	125 mL
½ cup	strawberries, cut into quarters or sliced into rounds	125 mL
½ cup	raspberries	125 mL
1 cup	packed trimmed spinach	250 mL
¼ cup	chopped walnuts	60 mL
¼ cup	crumbled blue cheese	60 mL

1. Pour vinaigrette into jar, wiping down any splashes on the side of the jar. Layer blueberries, strawberries, raspberries and spinach on top, loosely packing the spinach. Top with walnuts and blue cheese. Seal jar and refrigerate for up to 3 days.
2. When ready to serve, turn jar upside down in a bowl and let the dressing coat the salad.

Fig, Prosciutto and Mozzarella Salad

This trio of ingredients reminds me of my three boys. My oldest son, Eddie, loves prosciutto; my middle son, Murray, is the adventurous eater in our family, and figs with honey have become his favorite; and my youngest, Frankie, is a cheese freak. Put them together and you have a salad I adore, just like my boys.

**MAKES
1 SERVING**

Tip

This salad works just as well without the arugula. Just omit it and use a smaller jar (so you aren't tempted to overfill the jar with cheese).

- 1-quart (1 L) mason jar

2 tbsp	Balsamic Vinaigrette (page 164), made with reduced balsamic vinegar	30 mL
4	figs, quartered	4
1/4 cup	mini bocconcini (fresh mozzarella cheese)	60 mL
1 1/2 cups	packed arugula	375 mL
4	slices prosciutto	4

1. Pour vinaigrette into jar, wiping down any splashes on the side of the jar. Layer figs, bocconcini, arugula and prosciutto on top. Seal jar and refrigerate for up to 3 days.

2. When ready to serve, turn jar upside down in a bowl and let the dressing coat the salad.

Variation

Fig, Bresaola and Mozzarella Salad: Substitute 4 slices of bresaola for the prosciutto.

Breakfast Burrito in a Jar (page 13)

Chocolate Protein Smoothie (page 19)

Hummus Snack Pack (page 22)

Squash Soup with Yogurt and Chives (page 31)

Asian Vegetable and
Tofu Soup (page 36)

Watermelon, Feta and Arugula Salad (page 51)

Three-Tomato Pasta Salad with Pesto (page 67)

Fresh Spring Roll Salad with Sweet Dip Dressing (page 78)

Moroccan Couscous Salad (page 86)

Quinoa, Butternut Squash and Spinach Salad (page 89)

Roasted Salmon with Bibb Lettuce and Crispy Leeks (page 101)

Peach, Arugula, Mozzarella and Prosciutto Salad

There are many different delicious things going on in this salad. Peaches add sweetness, arugula shines with a peppery taste, prosciutto brings saltiness, and the mozzarella is smooth and velvety. Combined, they make an all-star salad.

Tips

Use peaches that are just about to ripen in this recipe. If they are really juicy, the juices will wilt the arugula.

Buy a ball of mozzarella cheese instead of a block, as it will be easier to tear into bite-size pieces for this salad. Gently pull the cheese apart with your hands.

- 1-quart (1 L) mason jar

1 cup	thinly sliced peaches	250 mL
1 tbsp	freshly squeezed lemon juice	15 mL
2 tbsp	Citrus Vinaigrette (page 166)	30 mL
2 cups	tightly packed arugula	500 mL
4 oz	mozzarella cheese, torn into bite-size pieces (see tip, at left)	125 g
4	slices prosciutto, loosely rolled	4

1. Place peaches in a medium bowl and drizzle with lemon juice, tossing to coat.
2. Pour vinaigrette into jar, wiping down any splashes on the side of the jar. Layer peaches, arugula, mozzarella and prosciutto on top. Seal jar and refrigerate for up to 3 days.
3. When ready to serve, turn jar upside down in a bowl and let the dressing coat the salad.

Citrus Salad with Fennel and Arugula

Just the name of this salad gets my mouth watering. With orange, grapefruit and lime, it delivers a triple punch of citrus. It's refreshing in the summer and offers a much-needed hit of vitamin C in the winter.

Tips

I prefer to use Marcona almonds in this recipe because they are rounder and plumper. You can buy them tossed in a bit of olive oil and salt. They are more flavorful in salads, but any almond will do.

If you don't plan on eating this salad within the first day, wrap the almonds in plastic wrap before placing them on top of the arugula. Before serving, unwrap the almonds and add them to the salad.

- 1-quart (1 L) mason jar

2 tbsp	extra virgin olive oil	30 mL
1 tbsp	unseasoned rice vinegar	15 mL
½ cup	chopped fennel bulb	125 mL
1	orange, sectioned (without pith)	1
1	large grapefruit, sectioned (without pith)	1
1	lime, sectioned (without pith)	1
2 cups	packed arugula	500 mL
¼ cup	Marcona almonds	60 mL
	Salt and freshly ground black pepper	

1. Pour oil and vinegar into jar, wiping down any splashes on the side of the jar. Layer fennel, orange, grapefruit, lime, arugula and almonds on top. Season to taste with salt and pepper. Seal jar and refrigerate for up to 3 days.
2. When ready to serve, turn jar upside down in a bowl and let the dressing coat the salad.

Variation

Heartier Citrus Salad: Add ¼ cup (60 mL) roughly grated ricotta salata cheese on top of the arugula for a heartier lunch.

Watermelon, Feta and Arugula Salad

This salad is one of my all-time favorites. Not only is it super-easy to prepare, but the combination of watermelon and feta, with a hint of fresh mint, makes it a refreshing summertime lunch.

**MAKES
1 SERVING**

Tip
Make sure to press the arugula down in the jar, leaving just enough room for the feta and mint at the top.

- 1-quart (1 L) mason jar

2 tbsp	extra virgin olive oil	30 mL
1 tbsp	balsamic vinegar	15 mL
	Salt and freshly ground black pepper	
1 cup	chopped watermelon	250 mL
2 cups	tightly packed arugula	500 mL
½ cup	crumbled feta cheese	125 mL
1 tbsp	chopped fresh mint	15 mL

1. Pour oil and vinegar into jar, wiping down any splashes on the side of the jar. Season to taste with salt and pepper. Layer watermelon and arugula on top, tightly packing the arugula. Top with feta and mint. Seal jar and refrigerate for up to 3 days.

2. When ready to serve, turn jar upside down in a bowl and let the dressing coat the salad.

BLT Salad

This salad version of the classic sandwich is simple and very good.

Tip

This salad works just as well with a vinaigrette dressing.

- Preheat oven to 400°F (200°C)
- Rimmed baking sheet, lined with foil
- 1-quart (1 L) mason jar

4	slices bacon	4
1	thick slice sourdough bread, cut into ½-inch (1 cm) cubes	1
1 tbsp	olive oil	15 mL
2 tbsp	Ranch Dressing (page 171)	30 mL
1 cup	halved cherry tomatoes	250 mL
1 cup	chopped romaine lettuce	250 mL

1. Arrange bacon on prepared baking sheet. Bake in preheated oven for 12 minutes or until crispy. Remove from oven and reduce oven temperature to 375°F (190°C). Let bacon cool completely, then break into pieces.

2. In a medium bowl, toss bread cubes with oil. Replace the foil on the baking sheet and spread bread cubes in a single layer on foil. Bake for 5 to 10 minutes, stirring occasionally, until golden brown. Let cool completely.

3. Spoon dressing into jar, wiping down any splashes on the side of the jar. Layer tomatoes, lettuce, bacon and croutons on top. Seal jar and refrigerate for up to 3 days.

4. When ready to serve, turn jar upside down in a bowl and let the dressing coat the salad.

Variation

Hearty BLT Salad: Add ½ cup (125 mL) cold chopped grilled chicken or shrimp, or cold chopped cooked lobster, before the croutons.

Chopped Brussels Sprout Salad

This is the salad version of a side dish I make for my family at Christmas. It's my sister, Sam's, favorite dish, and I usually make lots so I can send a few extra scoops home with her.

Tip

If you prefer, you can blanch the Brussels sprouts for a few minutes to soften them before adding them to the salad. Bring a large pot of salted water to a boil over high heat. Add Brussels sprouts and boil for 2 minutes or until vibrant green and slightly tender. Drain and plunge Brussels sprouts into a bowl of ice water to stop the cooking process. Remove from water after 1 minute and let cool completely.

- Preheat oven to 400°F (200°C)
- Rimmed baking sheet, lined with foil
- 1-quart (1 L) mason jar

2	slices bacon, chopped	2
¼ cup	pine nuts	60 mL
2 tbsp	extra virgin olive oil	30 mL
1 tbsp	freshly squeezed lemon juice	15 mL
2 cups	chopped Brussels sprouts	500 mL
¼ cup	chopped fresh dill	60 mL

1. Place bacon on prepared baking sheet. Bake in preheated oven for 12 minutes or until crispy. Remove from oven and reduce oven temperature to 375°F (190°C). Let bacon cool completely, then finely chop.

2. Replace the foil on the baking sheet and spread pine nuts in a single layer on the foil. Bake for 5 to 10 minutes, stirring occasionally, until golden brown. Check often, as they can burn quickly. Let cool completely.

3. Pour oil and lemon juice into jar, wiping down any splashes on the side of the jar. Layer Brussels sprouts, dill, pine nuts and bacon on top. Seal jar and refrigerate for up to 3 days.

4. When ready to serve, turn jar upside down in a bowl and let the dressing coat the salad.

Roasted Cauliflower Salad

Serve this salad with a chunk of crusty white bread and you'll feel like you are in a rustic Italian eatery. There's no need to add extra dressing; the juices from the roasted cauliflower and onions make it extra flavorful.

Tip

Reduced balsamic vinegar is fairly easy to find at grocery stores, but it's also easy to make your own. Pour 1 cup (250 mL) balsamic vinegar into a skillet and bring to a boil over medium-high heat. Reduce heat and simmer for 2 to 4 minutes or until thickened and syrupy. Remove from heat and let cool completely in the pan. It will continue to cook and thicken for a few minutes even off the heat.

- Preheat oven to 450°F (230°C)
- Rimmed baking sheet, lined with foil
- 1-quart (1 L) mason jar

2 cups	cauliflower florets	500 mL
1 cup	thinly sliced red onion	250 mL
½ cup	olive oil	125 mL
2 tbsp	reduced balsamic vinegar (see tip, at left)	30 mL
1 cup	rinsed drained canned chickpeas	250 mL
1 cup	packed arugula	250 mL

1. In a large sealable plastic bag or bowl, combine cauliflower, onion, oil and vinegar. Seal and shake to coat (or toss well in bowl). Arrange in a single layer on prepared baking sheet. Roast in preheated oven for 25 minutes or until golden. Let cool completely, then stir in chickpeas.

2. Spoon cauliflower mixture into jar and top with arugula. Seal jar and refrigerate for up to 3 days.

3. When ready to serve, turn jar upside down in a bowl and serve.

Variation

Sweet Heat Roasted Cauliflower Salad: Add ½ cup (125 mL) black currants and ½ tsp (2 mL) hot pepper flakes to the cauliflower mixture.

Green Goodness Salad

This is one of my mother's favorite salads. The combination of fresh spring peas and ricotta is magic. All you need is lemon, olive oil and freshly ground black pepper to finish them off.

Tip

This salad works best with full-fat ricotta, but light ricotta works too. I wouldn't use nonfat ricotta, as it's too hard and will weigh down the salad. A sloppy ricotta is ideal.

- 1-quart (1 L) mason jar

1 cup	fresh or frozen peas	250 mL
1 cup	diced Granny Smith apples	250 mL
2 tbsp	freshly squeezed lemon juice, divided	30 mL
2 tbsp	extra virgin olive oil	30 mL
1 cup	diced cucumber	250 mL
½ cup	ricotta cheese	125 mL
2 cups	packed mâche	500 mL
¼ cup	pistachios	60 mL
	Salt and freshly ground black pepper	

1. In a medium saucepan of boiling water, boil peas for 2 to 3 minutes or until tender. Drain and let cool completely.

2. Add apples and 1 tbsp (15 mL) lemon juice to a medium bowl of water and let stand for 5 minutes. Drain and pat dry.

3. Pour oil and the remaining lemon juice into jar, wiping down any splashes on the side of the jar. Layer cucumber, peas, apples, ricotta, mâche and pistachios on top. Seal jar and refrigerate for up to 3 days.

4. When ready to serve, turn jar upside down in a bowl and let the dressing coat the salad. Season to taste with salt and pepper.

Variation

Green Goodness Salad with Bacon: Cook 2 slices of bacon until crisp, then let cool and crumble. Place a piece of waxed paper on top of the salad and add bacon on top of paper. When serving the salad, remove the paper and bacon first, and sprinkle the bacon on top of the salad after seasoning it.

Beets, Mâche, Goat Cheese and Pistachio Salad

If I were selling this salad on a shopping network, it would be the showstopper! The combination of beets and goat cheese is simple but amazing. You could add a protein, such as chicken, but the salad definitely doesn't need it.

**MAKES
1 SERVING**

Tip

Beets have a terrific color, but they can stain clothing and hands. Wear disposable gloves when peeling them to avoid staining your hands.

- Preheat oven to 425°F (220°C)
- 1-quart (1 L) mason jar

2	purple beets	2
2	yellow beets	2
2 tbsp	Citrus Vinaigrette (page 166)	30 mL
1½ cups	packed mâche	375 mL
¼ cup	crumbled goat cheese	60 mL
¼ cup	pistachios	60 mL

1. Place beets on a sheet of foil, and wrap the foil around them, sealing the edges tightly. Roast in preheated oven for 1 hour or until tender. Let cool completely, then peel beets and cut into ¼-inch (0.5 cm) dice, keeping the two colors separate.

2. Pour dressing into jar, wiping down any splashes on the side of the jar. Layer purple beets, yellow beets, mâche, goat cheese and pistachios on top. Seal jar and refrigerate for up to 3 days.

3. When ready to serve, turn jar upside down in a bowl and let the dressing coat the salad.

Variation

Chopped Trout Beet Salad: Add ¼ cup (60 mL) cold flaked cooked trout on top of the mâche.

Raw Root Vegetable Salad

Raw root vegetables are no fun when cut into large bites, but when peeled into long strands and tossed together, the result packs a flavorful punch. Longer root vegetables, such as carrots and parsnips, are easiest to peel, but don't be afraid to try something new that you spot at the grocery store.

Tips

To peel the vegetables into strips, first use a vegetable peeler to peel off the outer skin and discard. Continue to peel the vegetable into ribbon-like strips, starting at the top and working your way down.

Blot the cucumber strips with paper towels to get rid of any excess water. You want the vegetables to be dry inside the jar so they don't water down the dressing.

- 1-quart (1 L) mason jar

2 tbsp	extra virgin olive oil	30 mL
2 tbsp	tahini	30 mL
	Juice of 1 lemon	
	Salt and freshly ground black pepper	
1	large carrot, peeled into strips (see tip, at left)	1
1	cucumber, peeled into strips	1
1	large parsnip, peeled into strips	1
1	large beet, peeled into strips	1
½ cup	packed arugula	125 mL
¼ cup	pistachios	60 mL
1 tbsp	unsalted sunflower seeds	15 mL

1. In a measuring cup, whisk together oil, tahini and lemon juice. Season to taste with salt and pepper.
2. Pour dressing into jar, wiping down any splashes on the side of the jar. Layer carrot, cucumber, parsnip, beet, arugula, pistachios and sunflower seeds on top. Seal jar and refrigerate for up to 3 days.
3. When ready to serve, turn jar upside down in a bowl and let the dressing coat the salad.

Variation

Hearty Root Vegetable Salad: Add ¼ cup (60 mL) cold shredded grilled chicken before the pistachios.

Butternut, Kale and Goat Cheese Salad

This salad may feel autumnal, but I eat it all year round. Kale is a perfect green for mason jar salads, as it stays firm even when sitting in dressing.

Tips

It's best to cut the kale leaves into fine slices, as big pieces are harder to eat and harder to stuff into the jar. To cut kale into chiffonade, cut out the tough stems and center ribs, stack several leaves together and roll them up into a cylinder. Cut the cylinder into thin slices.

For a crunchy finish, try topping the salad with ¼ cup (60 mL) roasted green pumpkin seeds (pepitas) or candied pecans, separating them from the goat cheese with parchment paper so they don't lose their crunch.

- Preheat oven to 425°F (220°C)
- Rimmed baking sheet, lined with foil
- 1-quart (1 L) mason jar

1 cup	cubed butternut squash (½-inch/1 cm pieces)	250 mL
1 cup	tiny broccoli florets	250 mL
1 cup	cherry tomatoes	250 mL
4 tbsp	olive oil, divided	60 mL
	Salt and freshly cracked black pepper	
1 tbsp	balsamic vinegar	15 mL
1 cup	sliced yellow bell pepper (½-inch/1 cm strips)	250 mL
1½ cups	packed trimmed kale leaves, cut into chiffonade (see tip, at left)	375 mL
¼ cup	crumbled goat cheese	60 mL

1. In a medium bowl, toss together squash, broccoli, tomatoes, 2 tbsp (30 mL) oil and salt and pepper to taste. Spread in a single layer on prepared baking sheet. Roast in preheated oven for 25 minutes or until caramelized. Let cool completely.

2. Pour the remaining oil and vinegar into jar, wiping down any splashes on the side of the jar. Layer yellow pepper, roasted vegetables and kale on top, tightly packing the kale. Top with goat cheese. Seal jar and refrigerate for up to 3 days.

3. When ready to serve, turn jar upside down in a bowl and let the dressing coat the salad.

Layered Caprese Salad

This classic Italian salad proudly displays the colors of the Italian flag (red, white and green). I like being a bit different, so I've added yellow tomatoes, but be your own caprese artist! If you make it during tomato season, the flavors in this go-to lunch staple are exceptional.

Tip
This salad is best kept simple. A drizzle of olive oil and balsamic vinegar is all it really needs, but any vinaigrette will do.

• **1-quart (1 L) mason jar**

2 tbsp	extra virgin olive oil	30 mL
1 tbsp	reduced balsamic vinegar (see tip, page 54)	15 mL
¾ cup	halved red cherry tomatoes	175 mL
¾ cup	halved yellow cherry tomatoes	175 mL
2 cups	packed arugula	500 mL
¼ cup	packed fresh basil	60 mL
1 cup	halved mini bocconcini (fresh mozzarella cheese)	250 mL
	Salt and freshly ground black pepper	

1. Pour oil and vinegar into jar, wiping down any splashes on the side of the jar. Layer red tomatoes, yellow tomatoes, arugula, basil and bocconcini on top. Seal jar and refrigerate for up to 3 days.

2. When ready to serve, turn jar upside down in a bowl and let the dressing coat the salad. Season to taste with salt and pepper.

Variation
Hearty Caprese Salad: Add ¼ cup (60 mL) cold chopped grilled chicken before the bocconcini.

Greek Salad

Greek salad is a true classic. It's great for lunch or dinner, on its own or with grilled lamb or chicken on the side. I'm not a huge fan of raw onion, so I always leave it out of my salads, but I've stuck with tradition and included it here for you.

Tip

Red peppers are an essential part of a Greek salad, but roasted red peppers work well too. If using roasted peppers from a jar, make sure to blot them on a paper towel before adding them to the jar.

- 1-quart (1 L) mason jar

2 tbsp	Greek Vinaigrette (page 167)	30 mL
1 cup	chopped red bell pepper	250 mL
1 cup	chopped cucumber	250 mL
¼ cup	thinly sliced red onion	60 mL
1 cup	halved cherry tomatoes	250 mL
½ cup	pitted halved kalamata olives	125 mL
1½ cups	packed arugula	375 mL
½ cup	cubed feta cheese	125 mL
1 tbsp	chopped fresh oregano	15 mL

1. Pour vinaigrette into jar, wiping down any splashes on the side of the jar. Layer red pepper, cucumber, onion, tomatoes, olives, arugula, feta and oregano on top. Seal jar and refrigerate for up to 3 days.

2. When ready to serve, turn jar upside down in a bowl and let the dressing coat the salad.

Variation

Hearty Greek Salad: Add 1 cold sliced grilled chicken breast or 3 cold grilled shrimp before the feta.

Fattoush

Fattoush is one of the best-known Middle Eastern salads. It's a chopped salad at heart, full of herbs and vegetables, and with toasted pita chips instead of croutons. Top it with a citrusy vinaigrette or even just freshly squeezed lemon juice and olive oil.

**MAKES
1 SERVING**

Tip

Most fattoush recipes fry the pita pieces so they become super-crispy. You can try this, but baking them works just as well.

- Preheat oven to 350°F (180°C)
- 1-quart (1 L) mason jar

1	6-inch (15 cm) pita	1
2 tbsp	olive oil	30 mL
2 tbsp	Citrus Vinaigrette (page 166)	30 mL
1 cup	diced cucumber	250 mL
½ cup	pomegranate seeds	125 mL
1 cup	halved grape tomatoes	250 mL
1 cup	chopped romaine lettuce	250 mL
¼ cup	crumbled feta cheese	60 mL
¼ cup	chopped fresh flat-leaf (Italian) parsley	60 mL
¼ cup	chopped fresh mint	60 mL

1. Brush both sides of pita with oil, then cut into 1-inch (2.5 cm) pieces. Spread pita pieces in a single layer on a baking sheet. Bake in preheated oven for 10 minutes, checking often, until golden brown. Let cool completely.

2. Pour vinaigrette into jar, wiping down any splashes on the side of the jar. Layer cucumber, pomegranate seeds, tomatoes, romaine, feta, parsley, mint and pita chips on top. Seal jar and refrigerate for up to 3 days.

3. When ready to serve, turn jar upside down in a bowl and toss to combine.

Pasta and Noodle Salads

Citrus Fregola Salad

Fregola is a type of pasta from Sardinia. It's similar to Israeli couscous and is perfectly suited to pasta salads.

Tip

Ricotta salata is a hard, salty ricotta cheese. It is sold in most cheese stores, but if you are having trouble finding it, use a crumbled hard feta cheese as a substitute.

- 1-quart (1 L) jar

4 cups	salted water	1 L
½ cup	dried fregola pasta	125 mL
2 tbsp	Citrus Vinaigrette (page 166)	30 mL
¼ cup	finely minced red onion	60 mL
½ cup	orange segments, pith removed	125 mL
½ cup	grapefruit segments, pith removed	125 mL
2 tbsp	roughly chopped fresh mint	30 mL
2 tbsp	roughly chopped fresh basil	30 mL
1 cup	packed arugula	250 mL
¼ cup	roughly grated or sliced ricotta salata	60 mL

1. In a medium pot, bring salted water to a boil over high heat. Add pasta and boil, stirring occasionally, for 8 minutes or until firm to the bite. Drain and let cool completely.

2. Pour vinaigrette into jar, wiping down any splashes on the side of the jar. Layer onion, pasta, oranges, grapefruit, mint, basil, arugula and ricotta salata on top. Seal jar and refrigerate for up to 3 days.

3. When ready to serve, turn jar upside down in a bowl and let the dressing coat the salad.

Variation

Vegetable Fregola Salad: Substitute ½ cup (125 mL) chopped cherry tomatoes for the oranges, and ¼ cup (60 mL) chopped zucchini for the grapefruit.

Orzo with Crispy Shallots and Feta Cheese

Orzo is rice-shaped pasta that lends itself to salads. It absorbs dressing perfectly, and its size makes it easy to spoon and eat. The key is making sure all the ingredients are spoon-sized, so you can get all the flavors in one bite.

MAKES 1 SERVING

Tips

Another method for fried shallots is to dredge the shallots in flour and fry them for 30 to 40 seconds over high heat.

It's best to not add the shallots to the orzo mixture until ready to eat. Place them on top of the spinach so they'll retain a bit of their crispness.

- 1-quart (1 L) jar

¼ cup	vegetable oil	60 mL
2	small shallots, thinly sliced into rounds	2
	Salt and freshly ground black pepper	
4 cups	salted water	1 L
½ cup	dried orzo pasta	125 mL
¼ cup	chopped drained oil-packed sun-dried tomatoes	60 mL
¼ cup	chopped pitted black olives	60 mL
3 tbsp	Citrus Vinaigrette (page 166)	45 mL
1 cup	baby spinach	250 mL
¼ cup	crumbled feta cheese	60 mL

1. In a medium saucepan, heat oil over low heat. Add shallots and cook gently, stirring occasionally, for 10 to 15 minutes or until crispy. Drain and let cool completely. Season to taste with salt and pepper.
2. Meanwhile, in a medium pot, bring salted water to a boil over high heat. Add pasta and boil for 8 minutes or until firm to the bite. Drain and transfer to a medium bowl. Let cool completely, fluffing the pasta so it doesn't stick together.
3. Add sun-dried tomatoes, olives and vinaigrette to the pasta, tossing to coat.
4. Layer pasta mixture, spinach, shallots and feta in jar. Seal jar and refrigerate for up to 3 days.
5. When ready to serve, turn jar upside down in a bowl.

Variation

Grilled Shrimp Orzo Pasta: Add 3 cold grilled shrimp on top of the orzo mixture before adding the spinach.

Penne with Asparagus Purée

This salad doesn't need any dressing, as the delicious asparagus purée coats the pasta perfectly.

Tips

Penne is my favorite for this salad, but any pasta shape will do. Try it with orecchiette, fusilli or any short pasta that helps scoop up the sauce.

If you can't find mini bocconcini, you can cut larger balls in half.

For added protein, when serving the salad, top it with 4 grilled shrimp.

The recipe makes more sauce than is needed for the salad; store the rest in the refrigerator for a few days to use with grilled chicken or fish.

- Blender
- 1-quart (1 L) jar

6	spears asparagus	6
4 cups	water	1 L
1 tsp	grated lemon zest	5 mL
¼ cup	extra virgin olive oil	60 mL
4 cups	salted water	1 L
½ cup	dried penne pasta	125 mL
¼ cup	chopped drained oil-packed sun-dried tomatoes	60 mL
1 cup	packed arugula	250 mL
¼ cup	mini bocconcini (fresh mozzarella cheese)	60 mL

1. Cut off the tips of the asparagus and set aside. Cut the asparagus spears into 1-inch (2.5 cm) pieces.

2. In a medium saucepan, bring water to a boil over high heat. Add asparagus pieces (but not the tips). Boil for 6 minutes or until tender.

3. Using a slotted spoon, transfer cooked asparagus to blender. Add lemon zest, oil and ½ cup (125 mL) of the cooking water; purée until smooth. Let cool completely.

4. Bring the remaining asparagus water back to a boil over high heat. Add asparagus tips and cook for 3 to 5 minutes or until tender-crisp. Drain, rinse with cold water and let cool completely.

5. Meanwhile, in a medium pot, bring salted water to a boil over high heat. Add pasta and boil, stirring occasionally, for 9 minutes or until firm to the bite. Drain and let cool completely.

6. Pour ¼ cup (60 mL) asparagus purée into jar, reserving the rest for another use. Wipe down any splashes from the side of the jar. Layer pasta, sun-dried tomatoes, asparagus tips, arugula and cheese on top of purée. Seal jar and refrigerate for up to 3 days.

7. When ready to serve, turn jar upside down in a bowl and let the purée coat the pasta.

Three-Tomato Pasta Salad with Pesto

Don't be fooled by the simplicity of this salad. Pesto, pasta and tomatoes are an awesome combination.

Tips

Microgreens are small and feathery, with a crazy-good flavor. They are usually sold in high-end grocery stores and specialty produce markets; if you can't find them, you can use any small leaf lettuce instead.

Tomatoes of any three colors will look beautiful in this recipe. Use any combination of colors that appeals to you — or whatever you can find at the grocery store.

- 1-quart (1 L) jar

4 cups	salted water	1 L
½ cup	dried penne pasta	125 mL
2 tbsp	pesto	30 mL
½ cup	sliced red cherry tomatoes	125 mL
½ cup	sliced orange cherry tomatoes	125 mL
½ cup	sliced yellow cherry tomatoes	125 mL
½ cup	microgreens (see tip, at left)	125 mL
¼ cup	freshly grated Parmesan cheese	60 mL

1. In a medium pot, bring salted water to a boil over high heat. Add pasta and boil, stirring occasionally, for 9 minutes or until firm to the bite. Drain, transfer to a bowl and let cool completely.
2. Add pesto to the cooled pasta and toss to coat.
3. Layer pasta mixture, red tomatoes, orange tomatoes, yellow tomatoes, microgreens and Parmesan in jar. Seal jar and refrigerate for up to 3 days.
4. When ready to serve, turn jar upside down in a bowl.

Variation

Chicken Pesto Salad: Add ½ cup (125 mL) cold sliced grilled chicken breast before the microgreens.

Gorgonzola Pasta Salad

This salad has few ingredients, but the combination of sun-dried tomatoes and Gorgonzola gives it a huge hit of flavor. You can add more vegetables if you like, but sometimes simple is best.

**MAKES
1 SERVING**

Tip

Gorgonzola works best if you crumble it when cold. Break it apart with your hands and add it to the jar. If you let it sit out at room temperature, it will get sticky and coat the salad, causing the lettuce to wilt over time.

- 1-quart (1 L) jar

4 cups	salted water	1 L
1½ cups	dried farfalle (bow tie) pasta	375 mL
2 tbsp	Citrus Vinaigrette (page 166)	30 mL
¼ cup	chopped drained sun-dried tomatoes	60 mL
1 cup	chopped seeded yellow and red tomatoes	250 mL
1 cup	baby spinach	250 mL
¼ cup	crumbled Gorgonzola cheese	60 mL
1 tsp	salt	5 mL
1 tsp	freshly cracked black pepper	5 mL

1. In a medium pot, bring salted water to a boil over high heat. Add pasta and boil, stirring occasionally, for 9 to 10 minutes or until firm to the bite. Drain and let cool completely.

2. Pour vinaigrette into jar, wiping down any splashes on the side of the jar. Layer sun-dried tomatoes, pasta, tomatoes, spinach and Gorgonzola on top. Seal jar and refrigerate for up to 3 days.

3. When ready to serve, turn jar upside down in a bowl and let the dressing coat the salad. Toss to combine. Season with salt and pepper.

Pasta Puttanesca Salad

If you know that *puttanesca* means "in the style of a whore," you may be wondering just what's in this dish. It's a simple combination of tomatoes, black olives, capers and anchovies. The origin of the name is unclear, although some sources say that, because the dish is easy to make quickly, it caused less interruption to a brothel's business. Regardless, it's delicious, so don't judge this pasta by its name.

**MAKES
1 SERVING**

Tips

Reduced balsamic vinegar is fairly easy to find at grocery stores, but it's also easy to make your own.
Pour 1 cup (250 mL) balsamic vinegar into a skillet and bring to a boil over medium-high heat. Reduce heat and simmer for 2 to 4 minutes or until thickened and syrupy. Remove from heat and let cool completely in the pan. It will continue to cook and thicken for a few minutes even off the heat.

If anchovies aren't your thing, just omit the anchovy paste.

- 1-quart (1 L) jar

4 cups	salted water	1 L
½ cup	dried penne pasta	125 mL
2 tbsp	extra virgin olive oil	30 mL
1 tbsp	reduced balsamic vinegar (see tip, at left)	15 mL
1 tsp	anchovy paste	5 mL
2	tomatoes, chopped	2
1 tsp	chopped oil-packed hot Italian peppers	5 mL
2 tbsp	drained capers	30 mL
¼ cup	chopped pitted black olives	60 mL
1 cup	packed arugula	250 mL
¼ cup	chopped fresh basil	60 mL

1. In a medium pot, bring salted water to a boil over high heat. Add pasta and boil, stirring occasionally, for 9 minutes or until firm to the bite. Drain and let cool completely.

2. In jar, whisk together oil, vinegar and anchovy paste. Wipe down any splashes on the side of the jar. Layer tomatoes, hot peppers, pasta, capers, olives, arugula and basil on top. Seal jar and refrigerate for up to 3 days.

3. When ready to serve, turn jar upside down in a bowl and let the dressing coat the salad.

Variation

Chicken Puttanesca Salad: Slice a cold grilled chicken breast and add it on top of the arugula.

Orecchiette Salad with Smoked Salmon, Chickpeas and Sage

I first tried this pasta when I visited Florence a few years back, and to this day I can't get it out of my head. It was so simple, but the flavor was out of this world. In Italy, it was served as a hot pasta dish, but tossed with some arugula, it makes for an impressive lunch.

**MAKES
1 SERVING**

Tips

When you add the smoked salmon to the warm pasta, the salmon might cook a touch. Don't worry if it does: it adds to the flavor of the dish.

The arugula will wilt when combined with the warm pasta. If you prefer your arugula crisp, add it right before serving.

• 1-quart (1 L) jar

3 tbsp	olive oil	45 mL
1	clove garlic, finely sliced	1
¼ cup	roughly chopped fresh sage	60 mL
4 cups	salted water	1 L
½ cup	dried orecchiette pasta	125 mL
½ cup	rinsed drained canned chickpeas	125 mL
¼ cup	chopped smoked salmon	60 mL
1 cup	packed arugula	250 mL
1	lemon wedge	1

1. In a small skillet, heat oil over medium heat. Add garlic and sage; cook, stirring, for 1 to 2 minutes to allow the garlic and sage to flavor the oil. Remove from heat and discard the garlic. Let oil cool completely.

2. In a medium pot, bring salted water to a boil over high heat. Add pasta and boil, stirring occasionally, for 9 minutes or until firm to the bite. Drain and let cool slightly.

3. Pour garlic oil into jar. Add warm pasta, chickpeas and salmon; seal jar and shake to combine. Remove lid and wipe down the sides of the jar. Add arugula and lemon wedge. Let cool completely, then seal jar and refrigerate for up to 3 days.

4. When ready to serve, remove the lemon wedge and turn jar upside down in a bowl, letting the garlic oil coat the salad. Squeeze the juice from the lemon wedge over top.

Variation

Orecchiette with Smoked Trout: Substitute ¼ cup (60 mL) cold flaked smoked trout for the salmon.

Pasta Salad with Tuna and Tomatoes

You can make a tuna pasta salad using only pantry ingredients — pasta, a can of tuna, a can of chopped tomatoes and a handful of capers — but I prefer to add fresh vegetables whenever possible.

Tip

For added flavor, use tuna packed in olive oil. Drain the tuna, but not completely, allowing the oil-soaked tuna to flavor the cooked pasta. Tuna is a protein that can stand being marinated in the dressing. If you are using tuna in oil, add it first and layer the other ingredients on top.

* **1-quart (1 L) jar**

4 cups	salted water	1 L
½ cup	dried fusilli pasta	125 mL
3 tbsp	extra virgin olive oil	45 mL
1 tbsp	white wine vinegar	15 mL
½ cup	chopped zucchini	125 mL
½ cup	chopped yellow summer squash	125 mL
½ cup	chopped cherry tomatoes	125 mL
¼ cup	chopped kalamata olives	60 mL
1 cup	packed mâche	250 mL
½ cup	drained canned tuna	125 mL

1. In a medium pot, bring salted water to a boil over high heat. Add pasta and boil, stirring occasionally, for 9 minutes or until firm to the bite. Drain and let cool completely.

2. Pour oil and vinegar into jar, wiping down any splashes on the side of the jar. Layer zucchini, summer squash, tomatoes, olives, pasta, mâche and tuna on top. Seal jar and refrigerate for up to 3 days.

3. When ready to serve, turn jar upside down in a bowl and let the dressing coat the salad.

Variation

Greek Pasta Salad: Substitute ¼ cup (60 mL) cubed or crumbled feta for the tuna.

Chicken Soup Pasta Salad

This is exactly what it claims to be: chicken soup in salad form. The flavors are simple but delicious, and it's an easy go-to any time of year. To make preparation easier, I usually buy a roasted chicken from the grocery store for dinner and use the leftovers in this salad.

MAKES 1 SERVING

Tip

For most lettuce salads, 2 tbsp (30 mL) dressing is plenty. For a noodle-based salad, 3 tbsp (45 mL) works better, as the pasta absorbs the dressing. It's all about personal taste, so try it both ways and see which you prefer.

- 1-quart (1 L) jar

4 cups	salted water	1 L
½ cup	dried farfalle (bow tie) pasta	125 mL
3 tbsp	Citrus Vinaigrette (page 166)	45 mL
1 tbsp	chopped fresh flat-leaf (Italian) parsley	15 mL
1 tbsp	chopped fresh thyme	15 mL
¼ cup	finely chopped red onion	60 mL
½ cup	chopped carrots	125 mL
½ cup	chopped celery	125 mL
1 cup	packed arugula	250 mL
½ cup	cold roughly chopped roasted chicken	125 mL

1. In a medium pot, bring salted water to a boil over high heat. Add pasta and boil, stirring occasionally, for 9 to 10 minutes or until firm to the bite. Drain and let cool completely.

2. Pour vinaigrette into jar, wiping down any splashes on the side of the jar. Layer parsley, thyme, onion, carrots, celery, pasta, arugula and chicken on top. Seal jar and refrigerate for up to 3 days.

3. When ready to serve, turn jar upside down in a bowl and let the dressing coat the salad.

Variation

Mock Chicken Soup Pasta Salad: Substitute ½ cup (125 mL) chopped firm tofu for the chicken.

Pasta Carbonara Salad

Carbonara is authentic Italian comfort food, with bacon, pasta and creamy eggs making it drool-worthy. My take uses the egg as a chopped protein, rather than as a sauce. It's got all the flavors, but is a lighter version for lunchtime.

MAKES 1 SERVING

Tip

A traditional carbonara has a good grinding of black pepper on top to give it some kick. You can add it on top of the salad when serving or layer it between the Parmesan and the bacon.

- Preheat oven to 400°F (200°C)
- Rimmed baking sheet, lined with foil
- 1-quart (1 L) jar

3	slices bacon	3
2	large eggs	2
4 cups	salted water	1 L
4 oz	dried spaghetti	125 g
2 tbsp	extra virgin olive oil	30 mL
1 tbsp	balsamic vinegar	15 mL
¼ cup	freshly grated Parmesan cheese	60 mL
1 cup	packed mesclun	250 mL

1. Arrange bacon on prepared baking sheet. Bake in preheated oven for 12 minutes or until crispy. Let cool completely, then roughly chop.

2. Meanwhile, place eggs in a small saucepan and cover with 2 inches (5 cm) of water. Bring to a boil over high heat. Turn the heat off and let stand for 15 minutes. Drain and run eggs under cold water. Remove shells and finely chop.

3. Meanwhile, in a medium pot, bring salted water to a boil over high heat. Add spaghetti and boil, stirring occasionally, for 7 to 8 minutes or until firm to the bite. Drain and let cool completely.

4. Pour oil and vinegar into jar, wiping down any splashes on the side of the jar. Layer eggs, Parmesan, bacon, spaghetti and mesclun on top. Seal jar and refrigerate for up to 3 days.

5. When ready to serve, turn jar upside down in a bowl and let the dressing coat the salad.

Variation

Asparagus Carbonara: Add ½ cup (125 mL) cooled cooked chopped asparagus before the eggs.

Spaghetti with Brussels Sprouts, Pine Nuts and Pancetta

The combination of pasta, pancetta and Brussels sprouts is a satisfying one. This salad is very simple to put together, with the Brussels sprouts leaves replacing lettuce.

**MAKES
1 SERVING**

Tip

An easy way to separate the Brussels sprout leaves is to first peel off and discard the first few tough leaves, then cut the sprout in half. Place the flat side down and, with your palm, press the leaves down. This loosens them up. Cut off the bottom of the sprout and separate the leaves.

Variation

Spaghetti with Brussels Sprouts and Cauliflower: Add ½ cup (125 mL) cooled roasted cauliflower on top of the spaghetti.

- Preheat oven to 375°F (190°C)
- Rimmed baking sheet, lined with foil
- 1-quart (1 L) jar

4 cups	salted water	1 L
4 oz	dried spaghetti	125 g
¼ cup	diced pancetta	60 mL
¼ cup	pine nuts	60 mL
4 cups	water	1 L
8 oz	Brussels sprouts, trimmed, halved and leaves separated	250 g
3 tbsp	Citrus Vinaigrette (page 166)	45 mL
¼ cup	chopped fresh flat-leaf (Italian) parsley	60 mL

1. In a medium pot, bring salted water to a boil over high heat. Add spaghetti and boil, stirring occasionally, for 7 to 8 minutes or until firm to the bite. Drain and let cool completely.

2. Meanwhile, in a medium skillet, over medium heat, sauté pancetta for about 8 minutes or until golden brown. Transfer pancetta to a plate lined with paper towels and let cool completely.

3. Spread pine nuts in a single layer on prepared baking sheet. Bake in preheated oven, stirring occasionally, for 5 to 10 minutes or until golden brown. Check often, as they can burn quickly. Let cool completely.

4. In the same medium pot, bring 4 cups (1 L) water to a boil over high heat. Add Brussels sprout leaves and boil for 30 seconds or until softened. Drain, transfer to a plate lined with paper towels and let cool completely.

5. Pour vinaigrette into jar, wiping down any splashes on the side of the jar. Layer pancetta, spaghetti, Brussels sprout leaves, pine nuts and parsley on top. Seal jar and refrigerate for up to 3 days.

6. When ready to serve, turn jar upside down in a bowl and let the dressing coat the salad.

Spring Pasta with Peas and Ham

You could use frozen peas any time of year to make this salad, but during the spring, fresh peas add a refreshing sweetness. It's worth waiting for.

Tips

When boiling the peas, do not add salt to the water. It will toughen them up. A pinch of granulated sugar, however, will add sweetness.

You can substitute ¼ cup (60 mL) chopped pancetta for the ham. Omit the olive oil and sauté the pancetta until crispy.

- 1-quart (1 L) jar

4 cups	salted water	1 L
½ cup	dried fusilli pasta	125 mL
1 tbsp	olive oil	15 mL
½ cup	diced ham	125 mL
2 cups	water	500 mL
½ cup	shelled peas	125 mL
3 tbsp	Citrus Vinaigrette (page 166)	45 mL
1 cup	packed arugula	250 mL
¼ cup	freshly grated Parmesan cheese	60 mL

1. In a medium pot, bring salted water to a boil over high heat. Add pasta and boil, stirring occasionally, for 9 minutes or until firm to the bite. Drain and let cool completely.

2. Meanwhile, in a medium skillet, heat oil over medium heat. Add ham and cook, stirring, for 5 minutes or until a golden crust forms. Let cool completely.

3. In the same medium pot, bring 2 cups (500 mL) water to a boil over high heat. Add peas and cook for 2 to 3 minutes or until firm and bright green. Drain and let cool completely.

4. Pour vinaigrette into jar, wiping down any splashes on the side of the jar. Layer pasta, peas, ham, arugula and Parmesan on top. Seal jar and refrigerate for up to 3 days.

5. When ready to serve, turn jar upside down in a bowl and let the dressing coat the salad.

Soba Noodle, Edamame, Corn and Tofu Salad

I was a soba noodle rookie for years. I avoided using them until my sister served me a variation of this salad. Now they are my go-to for noodle salads.

Tip

There are many ways to cook soba noodles, but however you do it, make sure you rinse them afterward to prevent stickiness and rinse off the starch.

● 1-quart (1 L) jar

4 cups	salted water	1 L
4 oz	soba noodles	125 g
2 cups	water	500 mL
½ cup	frozen edamame	125 mL
½ cup	corn kernels	125 mL
2 tbsp	Sesame Dressing (page 167)	30 mL
½ cup	chopped firm tofu	125 mL

1. In a medium pot, bring salted water to a boil over high heat. Add noodles and boil for 5 minutes or until firm to the bite. Drain, rinse with cold water and let cool completely.

2. Meanwhile, in another medium pot, bring 2 cups (500 mL) water to a boil over high heat. Add edamame and corn and cook for 3 minutes or until firm and brightly colored. Drain and let cool completely.

3. Pour dressing into jar, wiping down any splashes on the side of the jar. Layer noodles, edamame mixture and tofu on top. Seal jar and refrigerate for up to 3 days.

4. When ready to serve, turn jar upside down in a bowl and let the dressing coat the salad.

Variation

Soba Noodles with Shrimp and Edamame: When serving the salad, arrange 4 grilled shrimp on top.

Singapore Noodle Salad

This yummy salad is a deconstructed Singapore noodle dish. Instead of pan-frying the noodles, it's layered in a mason jar. I eat this at work or if I'm too hungry to cook when I get home.

Tip

It's best to soak the noodles in the dressing so they can absorb the traditional curry flavor, but if you'd prefer to decrease the intensity of the flavor, layer the green onions and red pepper on the bottom of the jar, then place the noodles on top.

- 1-quart (1 L) jar

1	large egg	1
1 tbsp	milk	15 mL
3 tbsp	vegetable oil, divided	45 mL
2 cups	water	500 mL
4 oz	rice vermicelli	125 g
1 tsp	grated gingerroot	5 mL
½ tsp	curry powder	2 mL
½ tsp	hot pepper flakes	2 mL
2 tsp	unseasoned rice vinegar	10 mL
¼ cup	chopped green onions	60 mL
¼ cup	chopped red bell pepper	60 mL
4	cold cooked medium shrimp	4
1 tbsp	soy sauce	15 mL
1 tbsp	chopped fresh cilantro	15 mL
1	lime wedge	1

1. In a medium bowl, whisk together egg and milk until blended.

2. In a small skillet, heat 1 tbsp (15 mL) oil over medium heat. Pour in egg mixture, tilting the pan to cover the bottom with a thin layer of egg. Cook for about 3 minutes or until almost set. Turn egg over and cook for 1 minute. Remove from heat and let cool. Once cool, roll egg into a cylinder and cut into thin strips.

3. In a medium saucepan, bring water to a boil over high heat. Add vermicelli and boil for 2 minutes or until tender. Drain, rinse thoroughly and let cool completely.

4. In a small bowl, whisk together ginger, curry powder, hot pepper flakes, the remaining oil and vinegar.

5. Pour dressing into jar, wiping down any splashes on the side of the jar. Layer vermicelli, green onions, red pepper, egg and shrimp on top. Pour in soy sauce and top with cilantro and lime wedge. Seal jar and refrigerate for up to 3 days.

6. When ready to serve, remove the lime wedge and turn jar upside down in a bowl, letting the dressing coat the salad. Squeeze the juice from the lime wedge over top.

Fresh Spring Roll Salad with Sweet Dip Dressing

My friend Mildred Piad makes the best Filipino fresh spring rolls. They are, frankly, amazing. The vegetables are slivered just right, and the proportions are perfect. She's tried for years to teach me, but mine just aren't as good. So I looked to her to help me create a version of her rolls in salad form. Our combined efforts turned out beautifully.

**MAKES
1 SERVING**

Tips

Be careful not to overcook rice noodles, or they will become mushy and stick together.

Cooked meat, such as the chicken in this recipe, should be eaten within 3 days of when it is cooked. If using leftover chicken, make sure its total storage time does not exceed 3 days.

Variation

Shrimp Spring Roll Salad: Omit the egg strips and chicken and substitute 4 cold chopped cooked shrimp.

• 1-quart (1 L) jar

1	large egg	1
1 tbsp	milk	15 mL
1 tbsp	olive oil	15 mL
2 cups	water	500 mL
4 oz	rice vermicelli	125 g
3 tbsp	Sweet Heat Dressing (page 168)	45 mL
½ cup	sliced red bell pepper	125 mL
½ cup	slivered carrots	125 mL
½ cup	bean sprouts	125 mL
¼ cup	slivered cucumber	60 mL
¼ cup	cold shredded rotisserie chicken	60 mL
¼ cup	chopped fresh cilantro	60 mL

1. In a medium bowl, whisk together egg and milk until blended.

2. In a small skillet, heat oil over medium heat. Pour in egg mixture, tilting the pan to cover the bottom with a thin layer of egg. Cook for about 3 minutes or until almost set. Turn egg over and cook for 1 minute. Remove from heat and let cool. Once cool, roll egg into a cylinder and cut into thin strips.

3. In a medium saucepan, bring water to a boil over high heat. Add vermicelli and boil for 2 minutes or until tender. Drain, rinse and let cool completely.

4. Pour dressing into jar, wiping down any splashes on the side of the jar. Layer red pepper, carrots, bean sprouts, cucumber, vermicelli, egg, chicken and cilantro on top. Seal jar and refrigerate for up to 3 days.

5. When ready to serve, turn jar upside down in a bowl and let the dressing coat the salad.

Cheater Pad Thai Salad

A typical pad Thai would have you stir-fry the noodles with the sauce, but I like to layer this deconstructed version. I also cheat the sauce by using my Sweet Heat Dressing.

Tips

To get more juice out of a lime, roll it on the countertop with the palm of your hand before cutting it into wedges. The rolling releases more juice.

For a heartier meal, add 3 cold grilled shrimp on top of the chicken.

Cooked meat, such as the chicken in this recipe, should be eaten within 3 days of when it is cooked. If using leftover chicken, make sure its total storage time does not exceed 3 days.

● 1-quart (1 L) jar

4 cups	water	1 L
4 oz	narrow rice noodles	125 g
3 tbsp	Sweet Heat Dressing (page 168)	45 mL
1/2 cup	thinly sliced red bell pepper	125 mL
1/4 cup	chopped green onions	60 mL
1 cup	shredded napa cabbage	250 mL
1/2 cup	bean sprouts	125 mL
1/2 cup	cold shredded cooked rotisserie chicken	125 mL
1/4 cup	chopped fresh cilantro	60 mL
1/4 cup	chopped unsalted peanuts	60 mL
1	lime wedge	1

1. In a medium saucepan over high heat, bring 4 cups (1 L) water to a boil. Add noodles and cook for 5 minutes or until tender. Drain, rinse thoroughly and let cool completely.
2. Pour dressing into jar, wiping down any splashes on the side of the jar. Layer noodles, red pepper, green onions, cabbage, bean sprouts, chicken, cilantro, peanuts and lime wedge on top. Seal jar and refrigerate for up to 3 days.
3. When ready to serve, remove the lime wedge and turn jar upside down in a bowl, letting the dressing coat the salad. Squeeze the juice from the lime wedge over top.

Grain and Legume Salads

Barley Salad with Apples, Dates and Parmesan

This salad is an awesome mix of contradictions. It's sweet and salty, it has fresh lettuce and comforting barley, and it feels wintery but is delicious in the summer. Try it and see if you can come up with your own lovable contradiction.

**MAKES
1 SERVING**

Tip

Dates are easy to find in most supermarkets, but if you are having a hard time, you can substitute dried apricots or dried figs.

- 1-quart (1 L) mason jar

¼ cup	quick-cooking barley, rinsed	60 mL
Pinch	salt	Pinch
¾ cup	water	175 mL
1 cup	chopped apples	250 mL
1 tsp	freshly squeezed lemon juice	5 mL
2 tbsp	Citrus Vinaigrette (page 166)	30 mL
¼ cup	finely chopped dates	60 mL
1 cup	packed arugula	250 mL
¼ cup	shaved Parmesan cheese	60 mL

1. In a small saucepan, combine barley, salt and water. Bring to a boil over high heat. Reduce heat to low, cover and simmer for 15 minutes or until water is absorbed. Remove from heat and fluff with a fork. Let cool completely.

2. Place apples in a medium bowl and drizzle with lemon juice, tossing to coat.

3. Pour vinaigrette into jar, wiping down any splashes on the side of the jar. Layer apples, dates, barley, arugula and Parmesan on top. Seal jar and refrigerate for up to 3 days.

4. When ready to serve, turn jar upside down in a bowl and let the dressing coat the salad.

Barley, Arugula and Cherry Tomato Salad

This is a crazy simple salad to make for lunch. The barley bulks it up, but the tomatoes and arugula make it feel light and fresh.

Tip

There are three types of barley: hulled, pot and pearl. Pearl barley is the most refined and cooks the fastest. It is most commonly associated with beef barley soup. Pot barley has been processed like pearl barley, but for a shorter time, so some of the bran remains. Hulled barley is the whole grain form, with only the outer husk removed; it is chewier and can take twice as long as pearl barley to cook.

• **1-quart (1 L) mason jar**

¼ cup	quick-cooking barley, rinsed	60 mL
Pinch	salt	Pinch
¾ cup	water	175 mL
2 tbsp	extra virgin olive oil	30 mL
1 tbsp	freshly squeezed lemon juice	15 mL
1 cup	chopped cherry tomatoes	250 mL
1½ cups	packed arugula	375 mL
½ cup	halved baby bocconcini (fresh mozzarella cheese)	125 mL
1 tsp	chopped fresh basil	5 mL

1. In a small saucepan, combine barley, salt and water. Bring to a boil over high heat. Reduce heat to low, cover and simmer for 15 minutes or until water is absorbed. Remove from heat and fluff with a fork. Let cool completely.

2. Pour oil and lemon juice into jar, wiping down any splashes on the side of the jar. Layer tomatoes, barley, arugula, bocconcini and basil on top. Seal jar and refrigerate for up to 3 days.

3. When ready to serve, turn jar upside down in a bowl and let the dressing coat the salad.

Variation

Hearty Barley and Arugula Salad: When serving the salad, top it with ½ cup (125 mL) sliced grilled chicken or 4 grilled shrimp.

Layered Tabbouleh Salad

This classic Middle Eastern salad is full of flavor. The traditional salad has all the ingredients mixed in a bowl. My version has them layered — mostly because it looks cool. Either way, it's yummy.

Tip

Roughly chopping the parsley instead of finely chopping it prevents it from getting too mushy in your salad.

- 1-quart (1 L) mason jar

1 cup	water	250 mL
½ cup	medium-grind bulgur	125 mL
Pinch	salt	Pinch
2 tbsp	Citrus Vinaigrette (page 166)	30 mL
¼ cup	finely chopped sweet onion	60 mL
½ cup	finely chopped cucumber	125 mL
½ cup	finely chopped tomatoes	125 mL
½ cup	finely chopped radishes	125 mL
¼ cup	finely chopped fresh mint	60 mL
½ cup	roughly chopped fresh flat-leaf (Italian) parsley	125 mL

1. In a small saucepan, bring water to a boil over high heat. Remove from heat and stir in bulgur and salt. Cover and let stand for 20 minutes. Drain off excess liquid and fluff bulgur with a fork. Let cool completely.

2. Pour vinaigrette into jar, wiping down any splashes on the side of the jar. Layer onion, cucumber, bulgur, tomatoes, radishes, mint and parsley on top. Seal jar and refrigerate for up to 3 days.

3. When ready to serve, turn jar upside down in a bowl and let the dressing coat the salad.

Variation

Tabbouleh Mezze: Add ¼ cup (60 mL) hummus and 1 crumbled falafel ball on top of the radishes. Seal jar and refrigerate for up to 1 day.

Bulgur Wheat Greek Salad

This is a basic Greek salad, but the addition of bulgur adds a nutty flavor and a ton of fiber.

Tip

There are a ton of vegetables in this salad, so you can make it with or without arugula.

- 1-quart (1 L) mason jar

1 cup	water	250 mL
1/2 cup	medium-grind bulgur	125 mL
Pinch	salt	Pinch
2 tbsp	Greek Vinaigrette (page 167)	30 mL
1/4 cup	finely chopped red onion	60 mL
1/2 cup	chopped cucumber	125 mL
1/2 cup	chopped red bell pepper	125 mL
1/2 cup	chopped tomatoes	125 mL
1 cup	packed arugula	250 mL
1/4 cup	pitted kalamata olives	60 mL
1/4 cup	crumbled feta cheese	60 mL
2 tbsp	chopped fresh dill	30 mL

1. In a small saucepan, bring water to a boil over high heat. Remove from heat and stir in bulgur and salt. Cover and let stand for 20 minutes. Drain off excess liquid and fluff bulgur with a fork. Let cool completely.

2. Pour vinaigrette into jar, wiping down any splashes on the side of the jar. Layer onion, cucumber, red pepper, tomatoes, bulgur, arugula, olives, feta and dill on top. Seal jar and refrigerate for up to 3 days.

3. When ready to serve, turn jar upside down in a bowl and let the dressing coat the salad.

Variation

Chicken Bulgur Greek Salad: Add 1/2 cup (125 mL) cold sliced grilled chicken on top of the olives.

Moroccan Couscous Salad

I absolutely love couscous, yet I never make it. When I was developing recipes for this book, I thought, "There has to be a simple salad version of this meal." Here's what I came up with — if I say so myself, it's pretty awesome.

Tip

If desired, you can sauté the carrots and zucchini beforehand to soften them up. Let cool completely before adding to the jar.

- 1-quart (1 L) mason jar

¾ cup	water	175 mL
¼ cup	couscous	60 mL
2 tbsp	Citrus Vinaigrette (page 166)	30 mL
¼ tsp	ground cinnamon	1 mL
¼ tsp	ground cumin	1 mL
¼ tsp	ground ginger	1 mL
½ cup	finely chopped carrots	125 mL
½ cup	finely chopped zucchini	125 mL
¼ cup	dried currants	60 mL
¼ cup	chopped dried apricots	60 mL
¼ cup	chopped dates	60 mL
½ cup	packed arugula	125 mL
¼ cup	sliced almonds	60 mL

1. In a medium saucepan, bring water to a boil over high heat. Stir in couscous, cover, remove from heat and let steam for 5 minutes. Fluff with a fork. Let cool completely.

2. In a small bowl, combine vinaigrette, cinnamon, cumin and ginger.

3. Pour spiced vinaigrette into jar, wiping down any splashes on the side of the jar. Layer carrots, zucchini, couscous, currants, apricots, dates, arugula and almonds on top. Seal jar and refrigerate for up to 3 days.

4. When ready to serve, turn jar upside down in a bowl and let the dressing coat the salad.

Variation

Chicken Couscous Salad: Add ½ cup (125 mL) cold chopped cooked chicken on top of the almonds.

Quinoa with Roasted Beets and Pomegranate

Pomegranate seeds are terrific in any salad. They are sweet and tart at the same time, and I love how they add a tiny burst of juiciness. Make sure to not pack this salad too tight, or the seeds will release their juice into the salad and not into your mouth!

**MAKES
1 SERVING**

Tips

The best way to seed a pomegranate is to cut it in half crosswise, stretch each half to loosen the seeds and whack the back of the fruit with a wooden spoon. All the seeds should fall out in seconds.

For extra protein, add ¼ cup (60 mL) finely cubed pecorino Romano cheese on top of the mâche.

- Preheat oven to 400°F (200°C)
- 1-quart (1 L) mason jar

2	large beets	2
¼ cup	quinoa, rinsed	60 mL
½ cup	water	125 mL
2 tbsp	Balsamic Vinaigrette (page 164), made with reduced balsamic vinegar	30 mL
½ cup	pomegranate seeds	125 mL
1½ cups	packed mâche	375 mL

1. Place beets on a sheet of foil, and wrap the foil around them, sealing the edges tightly. Roast in preheated oven for 1 hour or until tender. Let cool completely, then peel beets and cut into ¼-inch (0.5 cm) thick slices.
2. Meanwhile, in a small saucepan, combine quinoa and water. Bring to a boil over high heat. Reduce heat to low, cover and simmer for 15 minutes or until water is absorbed. Remove from heat and fluff with a fork. Let cool completely.
3. Pour vinaigrette into jar, wiping down any splashes on the side of the jar. Layer pomegranate seeds, beets, quinoa and mâche on top. Seal jar and refrigerate for up to 3 days.
4. When ready to serve, turn jar upside down in a bowl and let the dressing coat the salad.

Kale and Quinoa Salad

Kale and quinoa are superfood superheroes. Put them together and you have the all-star team of salads. Quinoa is full of protein and fiber, which makes it a great addition to any salad. Kale is a heartier leaf, so not only is it a healthy option, but it won't wilt over time.

MAKES
1 SERVING

Tip

Unlike other lettuces, kale can handle being sliced without wilting. First, cut off the tough stems and center ribs. Stack the leaves and roll them into a cigar shape, then slice them into strips. The thin slices will make the salad easier to eat.

- 1-quart (1 L) mason jar

¼ cup	quinoa, rinsed	60 mL
½ cup	water	125 mL
½	avocado, sliced	½
1 tsp	freshly squeezed lemon juice	5 mL
2 tbsp	Citrus Vinaigrette (page 166)	30 mL
¼ cup	chopped red onion	60 mL
½ cup	chopped cucumber	125 mL
½ cup	chopped red bell pepper	125 mL
1 cup	chopped trimmed kale leaves	250 mL
¼ cup	crumbled feta cheese	60 mL

1. In a small saucepan, combine quinoa and water. Bring to a boil over high heat. Reduce heat to low, cover and simmer for 15 minutes or until water is absorbed. Remove from heat and fluff with a fork. Let cool completely.

2. Place avocado in a small bowl and drizzle with lemon juice, tossing to coat.

3. Pour vinaigrette into jar, wiping down any splashes on the side of the jar. Layer red onion, cucumber, red pepper, quinoa, kale, avocado and feta on top. Seal jar and refrigerate for up to 3 days.

4. When ready to serve, turn jar upside down in a bowl and let the dressing coat the salad.

Variation

Barley and Kale Salad: Replace the quinoa and water with ½ cup (125 mL) cooked barley and skip step 1.

Quinoa, Butternut Squash and Spinach Salad

When I think of perfect food pairings, spinach and squash often go hand in hand. The addition of quinoa kicks it up a notch and makes this an easy staple for lunchtime.

Tip

Roasted squash works just as well in this salad. Toss the cubed squash with 1 tsp (5 mL) olive oil and 1 tsp (5 mL) fresh thyme, spread in a single layer on a rimmed baking sheet lined with foil and roast in a 450°F (230°C) for 15 minutes or until fork-tender.

- 1-quart (1 L) mason jar

¼ cup	quinoa, rinsed	60 mL
2½ cups	water, divided	625 mL
1 cup	cubed butternut squash	250 mL
2 tbsp	Basic Vinaigrette (page 164)	30 mL
¼ cup	finely chopped red onion	60 mL
1 cup	trimmed spinach	250 mL
¼ cup	crumbled feta cheese	60 mL
¼ cup	whole or chopped almonds	60 mL

1. In a small saucepan, combine quinoa and ½ cup (125 mL) water. Bring to a boil over high heat. Reduce heat to low, cover and simmer for 15 minutes or until water is absorbed. Remove from heat and fluff with a fork. Let cool completely.

2. Meanwhile, in a medium saucepan, bring the remaining water to a boil over high heat. Add squash and boil for 15 minutes or until fork-tender. Drain and let cool completely.

3. Pour vinaigrette into jar, wiping down any splashes on the side of the jar. Layer onion, squash, quinoa, spinach, feta and almonds on top. Seal jar and refrigerate for up to 3 days.

4. When ready to serve, turn jar upside down in a bowl and let the dressing coat the salad.

Herbed Rice Salad

This is a simple salad of rice and herbs. That's it. But sometimes that's all you need.

Tip

You can easily substitute brown rice or any other rice of your choice; adjust the cooking time and amount of water as indicated on the package.

- **1-quart (1 L) mason jar**

1 cup	water	250 mL
½ cup	long-grain white rice	125 mL
2 tbsp	Citrus Vinaigrette (page 166)	30 mL
1 tbsp	chopped fresh flat-leaf (Italian) parsley	15 mL
1 tbsp	chopped fresh basil	15 mL
1 tbsp	chopped fresh mint	15 mL

1. In a medium saucepan, bring water to a boil over high heat. Stir in rice, reduce heat to low, cover and simmer for 20 minutes or until rice is tender and water is absorbed. Remove from heat and fluff with a fork. Let cool completely.

2. Pour vinaigrette into jar, wiping down any splashes on the side of the jar. Layer parsley, basil, mint and rice on top. Seal jar and refrigerate for up to 3 days.

3. When ready to serve, turn jar upside down in a bowl and let the dressing coat the salad.

Variation

Herbed Feta and Rice Salad: Add ¼ cup (60 mL) crumbled feta cheese on top of the rice.

Basmati Asparagus Salad

This is one of the first salads I ever made in a mason jar, and I have made very few changes to it. I like it. It's a good lunch rice salad. But it's easy to add anything you like to it.

MAKES
1 SERVING

Tips

Consider saffron the diva of your spice cupboard. It's the most expensive spice in the world. You will only need 2 threads of saffron to flavor this small amount of rice.

Substitute ¼ cup (60 mL) halved mini bocconcini (fresh mozzarella cheese) for the feta cheese.

- 1-quart (1 L) mason jar

1½ cups	water, divided	375 mL
¼ cup	basmati rice	60 ml
Pinch	salt	Pinch
2	threads saffron	2
6	spears asparagus	6
2 tbsp	Balsamic Vinaigrette (page 164), made with reduced balsamic vinegar	30 mL
½ cup	chopped cherry tomatoes	125 mL
¼ cup	chopped niçoise olives	60 mL
¼ cup	crumbled feta cheese	60 mL
¼ cup	chopped fresh flat-leaf (Italian) parsley	60 mL

1. In a medium saucepan, bring ½ cup (125 mL) water to a boil over high heat. Stir in rice, salt and saffron, reduce heat to low, cover and simmer for 12 to 15 minutes or until rice is tender and water is absorbed. Remove from heat and fluff with a fork. Let cool completely.

2. Meanwhile, in a medium saucepan, bring the remaining water to a boil over high heat. Add asparagus, reduce heat to low, cover and simmer for 3 to 5 minutes or until tender-crisp. Remove asparagus from pan and plunge into a bowl of ice water; let cool completely. Cut into 1-inch (2.5 cm) long pieces.

3. Pour vinaigrette into jar, wiping down any splashes on the side of the jar. Layer tomatoes, olives, rice, asparagus, feta and parsley on top. Seal jar and refrigerate for up to 3 days.

4. When ready to serve, turn jar upside down in a bowl and let the dressing coat the salad.

Wheat Berry Salad with Blood Oranges and Feta

Wheat berries are wheat kernels that, when cooked, become chewy and tender. They are an easy add-on to mason jar salads because they are just as good cold as they are warm. Use them in any salad that calls for a grain like bulgur, rice or quinoa.

Tips

You could use less dressing in this salad, if desired, as the juice from the oranges will substitute for dressing.

The feta cheese can be replaced with queso fresco. It's milder in flavor, but works well with the citrus juices.

- 1-quart (1 L) mason jar

¼ cup	wheat berries	60 mL
1 cup	water	250 mL
2 tbsp	Citrus Vinaigrette (page 166)	30 mL
2	blood oranges, peeled, cut into rounds and quartered	2
1½ cups	packed arugula	375 mL
¼ cup	crumbled feta cheese	60 mL
¼ cup	chopped fresh mint	60 mL

1. In a medium saucepan, combine wheat berries and water. Bring to a boil over medium heat. Reduce heat to low, cover and simmer for 30 to 45 minutes or until wheat berries are tender. Drain and let cool completely.

2. Pour vinaigrette into jar, wiping down any splashes on the side of the jar. Layer blood oranges, wheat berries, arugula, feta and mint on top. Seal jar and refrigerate for up to 3 days.

3. When ready to serve, turn jar upside down in a bowl and let the dressing coat the salad.

Wheat Berry, Radish and Endive Salad

This is a crisp and clean salad. Radish and endive are one of those partnerships that work so well together. Add fresh lemon, and the flavor is amazing.

Tip

For a deeper flavor, toast the walnuts on a baking sheet in a 350°F (180°C) oven for 5 to 10 minutes or until golden brown. Check often, as they can burn quickly. Let cool completely.

- 1-quart (1 L) mason jar

¼ cup	wheat berries	60 mL
1 cup	water	250 mL
2 tbsp	extra virgin olive oil	30 mL
1 tbsp	freshly squeezed lemon juice	15 mL
	Salt and freshly ground black pepper	
½ cup	thinly sliced radishes	125 mL
½ cup	chopped escarole	125 mL
½ cup	sliced Belgian endive	125 mL
¼ cup	walnut halves (see tip, at left)	60 mL
¼ cup	shaved Romano cheese	60 mL

1. In a medium saucepan, combine wheat berries and water. Bring to a boil over medium heat. Reduce heat to low, cover and simmer for 30 to 45 minutes or until wheat berries are tender. Drain and let cool completely.

2. Pour oil and lemon juice into jar, wiping down any splashes on the side of the jar. Season to taste with salt and pepper. Layer radishes, wheat berries, escarole, endive, walnuts and cheese on top. Seal jar and refrigerate for up to 3 days.

3. When ready to serve, turn jar upside down in a bowl and let the dressing coat the salad.

Wild Rice Salad with Orange, Cranberries and Pecans

Wild rice is not actually rice but rather a long-grain marsh grass. It has a nutty flavor and a surprisingly chewy texture. It works beautifully in salads, and it doesn't get bloated from sitting in dressing.

Tip

To add more flavor to the wild rice, cook it in ready-to-use chicken or vegetable broth instead of water.

- 1-quart (1 L) mason jar

¼ cup	wild rice	60 mL
Pinch	salt	Pinch
¾ cup	water	175 mL
2 tbsp	Citrus Vinaigrette (page 166)	30 mL
1	orange, peeled, sliced into rounds and quartered	1
½ cup	dried cranberries	125 mL
1½ cups	packed arugula	375 mL
¼ cup	chopped pecans	60 mL

1. In a medium saucepan, combine wild rice, salt and water. Bring to a boil over high heat. Reduce heat to low, cover and simmer for 30 to 45 minutes or until wild rice is tender and water is absorbed. If rice still seems too crunchy when water is absorbed, add ¼ cup (60 mL) more water and cook until tender. Drain off any excess water, if necessary. Let cool completely.

2. Pour vinaigrette into jar, wiping down any splashes on the side of the jar. Layer oranges, cranberries, rice, arugula and pecans on top. Seal jar and refrigerate for up to 3 days.

3. When ready to serve, turn jar upside down in a bowl and let the dressing coat the salad.

Variation

Chicken Wild Rice Salad: Add ½ cup (125 mL) cold chopped grilled chicken on top of the arugula.

Lentil Salad with Tzatziki

Lentil salads are among the most satisfying salad options. They are so versatile, working well with everything from fish to meat to cheese. Canned lentils are great for creating quick lunch salads, but you can always cook dried lentils to use in their place, if you prefer.

Tip

Tzatziki is great for dips, or you can add dollops to chicken or fish, or use it to enhance vegetables and salads. For this salad, you can choose either full-fat or lower-fat tzatziki.

- 1-quart (1 L) mason jar

2 tbsp	tzatziki	30 mL
1 tbsp	extra virgin olive oil	15 mL
	Salt and freshly ground black pepper	
½ cup	chopped cucumber	125 mL
1 cup	rinsed drained canned lentils	250 mL
1 cup	packed arugula	250 mL
¼ cup	crumbled feta cheese	60 mL
¼ cup	chopped fresh dill	60 mL
1	lemon wedge	1

1. Spoon tzatziki into jar, then pour in oil, wiping down any splashes on the side of the jar. Season to taste with salt and pepper. Layer cucumber, lentils, arugula, feta, dill and lemon wedge on top. Seal jar and refrigerate for up to 3 days.

2. When ready to serve, remove the lemon wedge and turn jar upside down in a bowl, scooping out the tzatziki and dolloping it on top of the salad. Toss to coat, then squeeze the juice from the lemon wedge over top.

Variation

Chicken Lentil Salad with Tzatziki: Add ½ cup (125 mL) cold chopped grilled chicken before the feta.

Lentil Salad with Radicchio

Not only does the red color of radicchio pop against a plate of lentils, but the sweetness and crunch complements them, too. This is a fantastic salad to make for lunch any time of year.

Tips

You can combine the bacon mixture with the lentils instead of layering them.

For extra protein, add ¼ cup (60 mL) crumbled feta or goat cheese on top of the radicchio.

- 1-quart (1 L) mason jar

1 tbsp	olive oil	15 mL
3	slices bacon, finely chopped	3
¼ cup	finely chopped shallots	60 mL
¼ cup	finely chopped celery	60 mL
1 cup	chopped apples	250 mL
1 tsp	freshly squeezed lemon juice	5 mL
2 tbsp	Citrus Vinaigrette (page 166)	30 mL
1 cup	rinsed drained canned lentils	250 mL
1 cup	roughly chopped radicchio	250 mL

1. In a medium skillet, heat oil over medium-high heat. Add bacon, shallots and celery; cook, stirring, for 5 to 10 minutes or until vegetables are softened and bacon is starting to crisp. Using a slotted spoon, transfer bacon mixture to a plate lined with paper towels and let cool completely.

2. Place apples in a medium bowl and drizzle with lemon juice, tossing to coat.

3. Pour vinaigrette into jar, wiping down any splashes on the side of the jar. Layer bacon mixture, lentils, apples and radicchio on top. Seal jar and refrigerate for up to 3 days.

4. When ready to serve, turn jar upside down in a bowl and let the dressing coat the salad.

Santa Fe Salad

Beans are a great source of protein and fiber, and they make the perfect add-on to any salad. In this recipe, black beans, a staple of Mexican cuisine, are the highlight of the salad.

Tip

For a bit of a flavor boost, add ¼ cup (60 mL) finely chopped red onions on top of the red pepper. You can omit the green onions or add them as a garnish when serving.

Variation

Chicken Santa Fe Salad: Add ¼ cup (60 mL) cold shredded cooked chicken on top of the lettuce.

- Preheat oven to 400°F (200°C)
- Baking sheet, lined with foil
- 1-quart (1 L) mason jar

1	8-inch (20 cm) flour tortilla	1
3 tbsp	olive oil, divided	45 mL
¼ cup	roughly chopped avocado	60 mL
1 tbsp	freshly squeezed lime juice, divided	15 mL
½ cup	chopped red bell pepper	125 mL
½ cup	cooked or thawed frozen corn kernels	125 mL
½ cup	rinsed drained canned black beans	125 mL
¼ cup	chopped green onions	60 mL
1 tsp	finely chopped jalapeño pepper	5 mL
3 tbsp	finely chopped fresh cilantro	45 mL
1 cup	chopped romaine lettuce	250 mL
¼ cup	shredded Cheddar cheese	60 mL

1. Roll flour tortilla into a cylinder and cut into thin strips. In a small bowl, toss tortilla strips with 1 tbsp (15 mL) oil until coated. Arrange strips in a single layer on prepared baking sheet. Bake in preheated oven for 10 minutes or until golden brown. Let cool completely in pan.

2. Place avocado in a bowl and drizzle with 1 tsp (5 mL) lime juice, tossing to coat.

3. Pour the remaining oil and lime juice into jar, wiping down any splashes on the side of the jar. Layer red pepper, corn, beans, green onions, jalapeño, cilantro, avocado, lettuce and cheese on top. Place a parchment paper round on top of the cheese and top with tortilla strips. Seal jar and refrigerate for up to 3 days.

4. When ready to serve, remove tortilla strips and parchment paper, turn jar upside down in a bowl and let the dressing coat the salad. Top with tortilla strips.

Surf and Turf Salads

Fish Taco Salad

This salad combines two of my favorite things, salad and fresh tacos. It works with grilled or battered fish, or any protein you'd put in a taco. Have fun with it.

Tip

This salad works just as well with frozen battered fish. Follow the cooking instructions on the package, break into bite-size pieces and refrigerate until cold.

- Preheat broiler
- Rimmed baking sheet, lined with foil
- 1-quart (1 L) mason jar

6 oz	skinless halibut fillet	175 g
1 tbsp	olive oil	15 mL
	Salt and freshly ground black pepper	
½	avocado, chopped	½
1 tsp	freshly squeezed lemon juice	5 mL
2 tbsp	Avocado Lime Dressing (page 170)	30 mL
½ cup	chopped radishes	125 mL
1 cup	halved cherry tomatoes	250 mL
1½ cups	packed chopped romaine lettuce	375 mL
¼ cup	roughly chopped fresh cilantro	60 mL

1. Place halibut on prepared baking sheet. Brush both sides of fish with oil and season with salt and pepper. Broil for 8 to 10 minutes or until fish is golden and flakes easily when tested with a fork. Flake halibut into pieces and let cool completely.

2. Place avocado in a bowl and drizzle with lemon juice, tossing to coat.

3. Pour dressing into jar, wiping down any splashes on the side of the jar. Layer radishes, tomatoes, avocado, lettuce, cilantro and halibut on top. Seal jar and refrigerate for up to 3 days.

4. When ready to serve, turn jar upside down in a bowl and let the dressing coat the salad.

Variation

Seafood Taco Salad: Substitute 3 cold grilled medium shrimp, cut into pieces, for the halibut and skip step 1.

Roasted Salmon with Bibb Lettuce and Crispy Leeks

One word: Yum! I knew this combination of ingredients would taste good, but when I made it for the first time, it blew me away. The best part is that the leeks really do stay crispy for a few days!

MAKES 1 SERVING

Tips

Bibb lettuce is also known as butter lettuce or Boston lettuce.

In a pinch, you can substitute store-bought tzatziki for the Cucumber Dill Dressing.

Variation

Grilled Shrimp with Bibb Lettuce and Crispy Leeks: Substitute 3 or 4 cold poached or grilled medium shrimp for the salmon and skip step 1.

- Preheat oven to 450°F (230°C)
- Rimmed baking sheet, lined with foil
- Deep-fry thermometer
- 1-quart (1 L) mason jar

3 oz	skin-on salmon fillet	90 g
	Salt and freshly ground black pepper	
1	leek (white and light green parts only), sliced	1
1 tbsp	cornstarch	15 mL
1 cup	canola oil	250 mL
2 tbsp	Cucumber Dill Dressing (page 171)	30 mL
1 cup	chopped cucumber	250 mL
2 cups	packed Bibb lettuce (see tip, at left)	500 mL

1. Place salmon, skin side down, on prepared baking sheet and season with salt and pepper. Roast in preheated oven for 12 to 15 minutes or until fish is opaque and flakes easily when tested with a fork. Flake salmon into pieces, discarding skin if desired, then let cool completely.

2. Meanwhile, in a medium bowl, combine leek and cornstarch until coated.

3. In a medium saucepan over high heat, heat oil to 350°F (180°C) or until it starts to shiver. Add a handful of leeks and fry for about 30 seconds or until golden brown. Using a slotted spoon, transfer leeks to a plate lined with paper towels. Repeat with the remaining leeks, adjusting heat as necessary to prevent burning. Season to taste with salt and let cool completely.

4. Spoon dressing into jar, wiping down any splashes on the side of the jar. Layer cucumber, lettuce, salmon and leeks on top. Seal jar and refrigerate for up to 3 days.

5. When ready to serve, turn jar upside down in a bowl, scooping out the dressing and dolloping it on top of the salad.

Smoked Trout, Potato and Crème Fraîche Salad

Smoked trout is an exhilarating protein to add to a salad. It has a smoky and salty flavor that works well with potatoes and lettuce. You can buy it at most fishmongers and gourmet food stores.

Tips

If you have a hard time finding crème fraîche, you can replace it with sour cream.

If you can't find microgreens, you can substitute mâche or any other lettuce that is small, feathery and flavorful.

- 1-quart (1 L) mason jar

5	small new potatoes (about 1 inch/2.5 cm in diameter)	5
¼ cup	crème fraîche	60 mL
1 tbsp	extra virgin olive oil	15 mL
½ cup	halved yellow cherry tomatoes	125 mL
1½ cups	packed microgreens	375 mL
½ cup	roughly chopped smoked trout	125 mL

1. Place potatoes in a medium saucepan and cover with salted cold water. Bring to a boil over high heat. Boil for 15 minutes or until fork-tender. Drain and plunge potatoes into a bowl of cold water. Drain again, slice and let cool completely.

2. Spoon crème fraîche into jar, then pour in oil, wiping down any splashes on the side of the jar. Layer potatoes, tomatoes, microgreens and trout on top. Seal jar and refrigerate for up to 3 days.

3. When ready to serve, turn jar upside down in a bowl, scooping out the dressing and dolloping it on top of the salad.

Variation

Smoked Salmon Salad: Substitute 3 slices of folded smoked salmon for the trout.

Smoked Trout Lentil Salad

I'm a huge fan of smoked trout and adore adding it to just about anything. It works well with lettuce-based salads, but it's absolutely stunning with lentils. You must try this salad! I know you'll become a smoked trout junkie in no time.

Tip

If you prefer to use cooked dried lentils instead of canned, try cooking them in ready-to-use chicken broth for extra flavor. Just place ½ cup (125 mL) dried lentils in a saucepan, add enough broth to cover them by 1 inch (2.5 cm) and bring to a boil over high heat. Reduce heat and simmer for 15 to 20 minutes or until tender. Drain and let cool completely, then measure 1 cup (250 mL).

- 1-quart (1 L) mason jar

2 tbsp	Citrus Vinaigrette (page 166)	30 mL
¼ cup	finely chopped red onion	60 mL
½ cup	finely chopped carrots	125 mL
½ cup	finely chopped celery	125 mL
1 cup	rinsed drained canned lentils	250 mL
1 cup	packed mâche	250 mL
½ cup	roughly chopped smoked trout	125 mL
1 tbsp	chopped fresh thyme	15 mL

1. Pour vinaigrette into jar, wiping down any splashes on the side of the jar. Layer onion, carrots, celery, lentils, mâche, trout and thyme on top. Seal jar and refrigerate for up to 3 days.

2. When ready to serve, turn jar upside down in a bowl and let the dressing coat the salad.

Variation

Smoked Salmon Lentil Salad: Substitute 2 tbsp (30 mL) chopped fresh dill for the thyme, and ¼ cup (60 mL) roughly chopped smoked salmon for the trout.

Tuna Salad, Deli Style

One of my favorite salads, offered up at most delis, is simply a scoop of tuna on top of lettuce and vegetables. It's nothing fancy, but it's so good. I added pickles here, for a personal twist, but it's just as tasty without them.

Tips

The tuna salad mixture makes about 1 cup (250 mL). You can use half of that in this salad and keep the leftovers for a snack, or to make a sandwich or tuna melt.

If you want the tuna to be on top of the salad, place a piece of parchment paper over the lettuce and scoop the tuna on top. When ready to serve, pull the parchment paper with the tuna out of the jar, pour the salad into a bowl and place the tuna on top.

For variety, you can replace the scoop of tuna salad with your favorite egg, salmon or chicken salad.

- 1-quart (1 L) mason jar

1	can (6 oz/170 g) flaked white tuna in water, drained	1
1 tsp	finely chopped fresh dill	5 mL
1 tsp	finely chopped green onion	5 mL
1 tbsp	mayonnaise	15 mL
1 tsp	freshly squeezed lemon juice	5 mL
	Salt and freshly ground black pepper	
2 tbsp	Basic Vinaigrette (page 164)	30 mL
½ cup	chopped cucumber	125 mL
½ cup	halved cherry tomatoes	125 mL
¼ cup	finely chopped celery	60 mL
½ cup	finely chopped green bell pepper	125 mL
¼ cup	finely chopped dill pickles	60 mL
1 cup	roughly chopped iceberg lettuce	250 mL

1. In a medium bowl, combine tuna, dill, onion, mayonnaise and lemon juice until smooth. Season to taste with salt and pepper.
2. Pour vinaigrette into jar, wiping down any splashes on the side of the jar. Layer cucumber, tomatoes, celery, green pepper, pickles, lettuce and a scoop of tuna salad. Seal jar and refrigerate for up to 3 days.
3. When ready to serve, turn jar upside down in a bowl and let the dressing coat the salad.

Tuna "Melt" Salad

This is my deconstructed version of a tuna melt sandwich, turned into a salad. It might sound odd, but it's delicious.

Tips

This salad also works well with prepared tuna salad in place of plain drained tuna.

If desired, you can use the homemade croutons from the Chicken Caesar Salad (page 112).

• **1-quart (1 L) mason jar**

2 tbsp	Ranch Dressing (page 171)	30 mL
1 cup	chopped cucumber	250 mL
½ cup	chopped carrots	125 mL
½ cup	chopped celery	125 mL
1½ cups	packed chopped iceberg lettuce	375 mL
1	can (6 oz/170 g) solid white tuna in water, drained	1
1 tbsp	chopped fresh parsley	15 mL
½ cup	shredded Cheddar cheese	125 mL
½ cup	croutons	125 mL

1. Pour dressing into jar, wiping down any splashes on the side of the jar. Layer cucumber, carrots, celery, lettuce, tuna, parsley, cheese and croutons on top. Seal jar and refrigerate for up to 3 days.

2. When ready to serve, turn jar upside down in a bowl and let the dressing coat the salad.

Variation

Crab Melt Salad: Substitute canned backfin (lump) crabmeat, drained, for the tuna.

Niçoise Salad

If you want to transport yourself to the south of France over lunch, bring a packed niçoise salad. Be sure to use local, fresh ingredients for maximum flavor. I like to use a simple dressing of olive oil and lemon juice to let the other flavors in the salad shine through.

Tip
Bibb lettuce is also known as butter lettuce or Boston lettuce.

• **1-quart (1 L) mason jar**

5	small new potatoes (about 1 inch/2.5 cm in diameter)	5
1	large egg	1
1 cup	trimmed green beans	250 mL
1 cup	water	250 mL
2 tbsp	extra virgin olive oil	30 mL
1 tbsp	freshly squeezed lemon juice	15 mL
½ cup	chopped plum (Roma) tomatoes	125 mL
1 cup	packed Bibb lettuce (see tip, at left)	250 mL
1	can (6 oz/170 g) solid white tuna in water, drained	1
¼ cup	pitted niçoise or other black olives	60 mL
1	sprig fresh thyme, leaves chopped	1

1. Place potatoes in a medium saucepan and cover with salted cold water. Bring to a boil over high heat. Boil for 15 minutes or until fork-tender. Drain and plunge potatoes into a bowl of cold water. Drain again, slice and let cool completely.

2. Meanwhile, place egg in a small saucepan and cover with 2 inches (5 cm) of water. Bring to a boil over high heat. Turn the heat off and let stand for 15 minutes. Drain and run egg under cold water. Remove shells and cut into quarters.

3. In the same medium saucepan, bring 1 cup (250 mL) water to a boil over high heat. Add green beans, reduce heat to low, cover and simmer for 3 to 5 minutes or until tender-crisp. Remove beans from pan and plunge into a bowl of ice water; let cool completely. Drain and cut into 1-inch (2.5 cm) long pieces.

Tip

Although they are part of the classic salad, I've left anchovies out here. If you'd like to include them, add 1 tsp (5 mL) chopped anchovies on top of the tuna. If you want the salty taste but not the anchovies, add 1 tsp (5 mL) drained capers on top of the tuna.

4. Pour oil and lemon juice into jar, wiping down any splashes on the side of the jar. Layer green beans, tomatoes, potatoes, lettuce, tuna, olives and egg on top. Sprinkle with thyme. Seal jar and refrigerate for up to 3 days.

5. When ready to serve, turn jar upside down in a bowl and let the dressing coat the salad.

Variation

Grilled Tuna Niçoise Salad: Substitute 4 oz (125 g) cold sliced grilled tuna for the canned tuna.

Tuna, White Bean and Arugula Salad

My husband, Mike, is a creature of habit. Every weekend, I stockpile the refrigerator with all the fabulous salads from this book, and the only one he wants is this one. So I make different ones for me and this salad for him. I have to admit, it's easy to make, easy to eat over and over again and healthy, too!

Tip

This salad works with just about any leftover vegetables you have in the refrigerator. You can add up to ½ cup (125 mL) chopped vegetables, such as carrots, bell peppers or fennel bulb.

- 1-quart (1 L) mason jar

2 tbsp	Lemon Dijon Dressing (page 169)	30 mL
½ cup	chopped celery	125 mL
1 cup	chopped cucumber	250 mL
½ cup	rinsed drained canned white beans	125 mL
1 cup	tightly packed arugula	250 mL
1	small can (3 oz/85 g) solid white tuna in water, drained	1

1. Pour dressing into jar, wiping down any splashes on the side of the jar. Layer celery, cucumber, beans, arugula and tuna on top. Seal jar and refrigerate for up to 3 days.

2. When ready to serve, turn jar upside down in a bowl and let the dressing coat the salad.

Variation

Salmon, White Bean and Arugula Salad: Substitute drained canned salmon or cold flaked roasted salmon for the tuna.

Lobster Roll Salad

My husband and I and our three boys vacation in Nantucket every year. It's our happy place. While we are there, I try to eat a lobster roll every day. This is my version of my favorite sandwich in salad form.

Tips

Bibb lettuce is also known as butter lettuce or Boston lettuce.

If you're worried about the toasts getting soggy in the jar, you can store them in a separate jar or airtight container instead.

- Preheat oven to 375°F (190°C)
- 1-quart (1 L) mason jar

1	small egg bun, cut into 3 slices	1
1 tbsp	butter	15 mL
2 tbsp	mayonnaise	30 mL
1 tsp	Dijon mustard	5 mL
1 tsp	white vinegar	5 mL
	Salt and freshly ground black pepper	
1 cup	chopped celery	250 mL
½ cup	chopped radishes	125 mL
¼ cup	finely chopped fresh dill	60 mL
1½ cups	packed roughly ripped Bibb lettuce (see tip, at left)	375 mL
1 cup	drained thawed frozen cooked chopped lobster	250 mL

1. Butter both sides of bun slices and place on a baking sheet. Toast in preheated oven for 5 minutes, checking to make sure they don't get too brown. Turn bread over and toast for 5 minutes or until lightly browned on both sides. Let cool completely.

2. In a medium bowl, combine mayonnaise, mustard and vinegar. Season to taste with salt and pepper.

3. Spoon dressing into jar, wiping down any splashes on the side of the jar. Layer celery, radishes, dill, lettuce and lobster on top. Place a parchment paper round on top of the lobster and top with toasts. Seal jar and refrigerate for up to 3 days.

4. When ready to serve, remove parchment paper and toasts. Turn jar upside down in a bowl, scooping out the dressing and dolloping it on top of the salad. Top with toasts.

Variation

Crab Roll Salad: Substitute thawed frozen backfin (lump) crabmeat for the lobster.

Shrimp Cocktail Salad

This salad is a simple take on the classic appetizer. Instead of using a traditional thick cocktail sauce, fresh tomatoes and grated horseradish add flavor and heat to this portable lunch. I prefer a simple dressing of lemon juice and olive oil to let the fresh horseradish shine.

MAKES
MAKES **1 SERVING**

Tips

For a heartier dressing, mix the olive oil with 1 tbsp (15 mL) classic cocktail sauce.

If you like a spicier lettuce, substitute arugula for the romaine.

If you don't have fresh horseradish available, use 1 tsp (5 mL) prepared horseradish, adding it before the cucumber.

- 1-quart (1 L) mason jar

3 cups	water	750 mL
5	medium shrimp, peeled and deveined	5
½	avocado, diced	½
2	lemon wedges, divided	2
2 tbsp	extra virgin olive oil	30 mL
1 cup	chopped cucumber	250 mL
1 cup	halved red and yellow cherry tomatoes	250 mL
1½ cups	chopped romaine lettuce	375 mL
1 tbsp	grated peeled horseradish	15 mL

1. In a medium saucepan, bring water to a boil over high heat. Add shrimp and cook for 3 minutes or until pink, firm and opaque. Drain and let cool completely, then cut each shrimp into 3 pieces.

2. Place avocado in a bowl and squeeze the juice from 1 lemon wedge over top, tossing to coat.

3. Pour oil into jar, wiping down any splashes on the side of the jar. Layer cucumber, tomatoes, lettuce, horseradish, shrimp, avocado and the remaining lemon wedge on top. Seal jar and refrigerate for up to 3 days.

4. When ready to serve, remove lemon wedge, turn jar upside down in a bowl and let the oil coat the salad. Squeeze the juice from the lemon wedge over top.

Shrimp, Edamame and Pea Shoot Salad

Pea shoots are a great addition to any salad, contributing just the right amount of crunch. They also offer vitamins C and A, plus a small hit of high-quality protein. This is a great summer salad, but it's really just as good any time of year.

**MAKES
1 SERVING**

Tips

Pea shoots will last for a few days in a sealed mason jar, but they are delicate, so they definitely need to be eaten within those few days.

For a creamy finish, add ¼ avocado, chopped and tossed with a squeeze of fresh lemon juice, on top of the shrimp.

- 1-quart (1 L) mason jar

3 cups	water	750 mL
5	medium shrimp, peeled and deveined	5
2 tbsp	extra virgin olive oil	30 mL
1 tbsp	unseasoned rice vinegar	15 mL
	Salt and freshly cracked black pepper	
1 cup	chopped cucumber	250 mL
½ cup	chopped yellow bell pepper	125 mL
½ cup	julienned carrots (see tip, page 36)	125 mL
½ cup	cooked edamame	125 mL
1 cup	pea shoots	250 mL

1. In a medium saucepan, bring water to a boil over high heat. Add shrimp and cook for 3 minutes or until pink, firm and opaque. Drain and let cool completely, then cut into small pieces.

2. Pour oil and vinegar into jar, wiping down any splashes on the side of the jar. Season to taste with salt and pepper. Layer cucumber, yellow pepper, carrots, edamame, pea shoots and shrimp on top. Seal jar and refrigerate for up to 3 days.

3. When ready to serve, turn jar upside down in a bowl and let the dressing coat the salad.

Chicken Caesar Salad

This salad is a classic. It never goes out of style. I love the traditional dressing, but it works well with just about any other dressing, too. Have fun with it and make it your own.

**MAKES
1 SERVING**

Tip

I'm a big fan of cooking bacon in the oven. It stays flat, it doesn't mess up your stove and counter, and it's always perfectly crispy.

- Preheat oven to 400°F (200°C)
- Rimmed baking sheet, lined with foil
- 1-quart (1 L) mason jar

3 cups	water	750 mL
5	thyme sprigs	5
1	bay leaf	1
1	boneless skinless chicken breast (about 4 oz/125 g)	1
6	baguette slices	6
2 tbsp	olive oil	30 mL
	Salt and freshly ground black pepper	
2	slices bacon	2
2 tbsp	Creamy Caesar Dressing (page 173)	30 mL
½ cup	halved cherry tomatoes	125 mL
2 cups	chopped romaine lettuce	500 mL
¼ cup	freshly grated Parmesan cheese	60 mL
1	lemon wedge	1

1. In a medium saucepan, bring water to a boil over high heat. Add thyme, bay leaf and chicken. Reduce heat to low, cover and simmer for 15 minutes or until chicken is no longer pink inside. Transfer chicken to a cutting board and discard herbs. Let chicken cool completely, then slice.

2. Meanwhile, place baguette slices on prepared baking sheet. Brush both sides of bread with oil and season with salt and pepper. Bake in preheated oven for 10 minutes, turning once, until browned on both sides. Remove from oven, leaving oven on. Remove bread from pan and let cool completely, then break apart into rough pieces.

3. Place bacon on the baking sheet. Bake for 12 minutes or until crispy. Let cool completely, then break into rough pieces.

Tip

Although tomatoes are not a traditional part of a classic Caesar salad, using a hearty vegetable on the bottom prevents the lettuce from getting soggy. You could use chopped cucumber instead, if you prefer.

4. Spoon dressing into jar, wiping down any splashes on the side of the jar. Season to taste with salt and pepper. Layer tomatoes, lettuce, chicken, bacon, Parmesan and croutons on top. Wrap lemon wedge in plastic wrap and place on top. Seal jar and refrigerate for up to 3 days.

5. When ready to serve, remove the lemon wedge and place jar upside down in a bowl, scooping out the dressing and dolloping it on top of the salad. Toss to coat salad with dressing. Squeeze the juice from the lemon wedge over top.

Variation

Grilled Shrimp Caesar Salad: Substitute 3 cold grilled shrimp, cut into pieces, for the chicken and skip step 1.

Classic Cobb Salad

This is the quintessential American salad. It is said to have originated at the Brown Derby restaurant in Los Angeles in the 1930s. Eighty-five years later, little about it has changed. For those of you, like my husband, who don't like blue cheese, swap it out for something else crumbly, such as goat cheese, or for shredded Cheddar cheese.

**MAKES
1 SERVING**

Tips

Iceberg is the traditional lettuce for this salad, but another crunchy option, such as Belgian endive or escarole, would work just as well.

For a lighter dressing, substitute Balsamic Vinaigrette (page 164).

Blue Cheese and Chive Dressing (page 170) is another great option for this salad. If using it, replace the blue cheese in the salad with a hard cheese, such as shredded Cheddar.

Cooked meat, such as the chicken in this recipe, should be eaten within 3 days of when it is cooked. If using leftover chicken, make sure its total storage time does not exceed 3 days.

- Preheat oven to 400°F (200°C)
- Rimmed baking sheet, lined with foil
- 1-quart (1 L) mason jar

2	large eggs	2
4	slices bacon	4
½ cup	diced avocado	125 mL
1 tsp	freshly squeezed lemon juice	5 mL
2 tbsp	Ranch Dressing (page 171)	30 mL
1 cup	chopped yellow bell pepper	250 mL
1 cup	sliced baby cucumbers	250 mL
½ cup	halved cherry tomatoes	125 mL
1 cup	sliced iceberg lettuce	250 mL
½ cup	cold shredded cooked chicken	125 mL
¼ cup	crumbled blue cheese	60 mL

1. Place eggs in a small saucepan and cover with 2 inches (5 cm) of water. Bring to a boil over high heat. Turn the heat off and let stand for 15 minutes. Drain and run eggs under cold water. Remove shells and cut into quarters.
2. Meanwhile, arrange bacon on prepared baking sheet. Bake in preheated oven for 12 minutes or until crispy. Let cool completely, then break into pieces.
3. Place avocado in a bowl and drizzle with lemon juice, tossing to coat.
4. Pour dressing into jar, wiping down any splashes on the side of the jar. Layer yellow pepper, cucumbers, tomatoes, lettuce, avocado, chicken, eggs, bacon and blue cheese on top. Seal jar and refrigerate for up to 3 days.
5. When ready to serve, turn jar upside down in a bowl and let the dressing coat the salad.

Chicken, New Potato and Thyme Salad

This is a great summer picnic salad. Typically, this combination works with a creamy dressing, but this salad allows for the potatoes to marinate in a vinaigrette for added flavor.

Tips

You can use jarred roasted peppers in this recipe or roast your own. To roast your own, preheat oven to 400°F (200°C). Lay peppers on their side on a baking sheet lined with foil and roast for 40 minutes, turning once, until skin is blackened. Transfer to a heatproof bowl and cover with plastic wrap. When cool enough to handle, scrape off the blackened skins with the back of a knife.

I use rotisserie chicken for convenience, but you can just as easily use grilled, roasted or poached chicken in this recipe.

- 1-quart (1 L) mason jar

6	small new potatoes (about 1 inch/2.5 cm in diameter)	6
2 tbsp	Citrus Vinaigrette (see page 166)	30 mL
¼ cup	chopped roasted red bell pepper	60 mL
½ cup	cold shredded rotisserie chicken	125 mL
1 cup	packed mâche	250 mL
1 tbsp	chopped fresh thyme	15 mL

1. Place potatoes in a medium saucepan and cover with salted cold water. Bring to a boil over high heat. Boil for 15 minutes or until fork-tender. Drain and plunge potatoes into a bowl of cold water. Drain again, cut in half and let cool completely.

2. Pour vinaigrette into jar, wiping down any splashes on the side of the jar. Layer potatoes, roasted pepper, chicken, mâche and thyme on top. Seal jar and refrigerate for up to 3 days.

3. When ready to serve, turn jar upside down in a bowl and let the dressing coat the salad.

Chef Salad

This salad is hardly hip, but it's really, really good. There's nothing else to say, except that it's a classic. And one very well suited to a mason jar.

Tips

I like using iceberg — it seems "old school" — but you could hip up this salad with just about any greens you like. Try to pick a firmer lettuce, as feathery types will flatten with the weight of the cheese and egg.

Try using different chopped cooked meats in this salad, such as roast beef or Genoa salami.

- 1-quart (1 L) mason jar

1	large egg	1
2 tbsp	Herb Vinaigrette (page 165)	30 mL
1 cup	chopped cucumber	250 mL
½ cup	chopped cooked turkey	125 mL
½ cup	chopped cooked ham	125 mL
1 cup	chopped iceberg lettuce	250 mL
¼ cup	shredded Swiss cheese	60 mL

1. Place egg in a small saucepan and cover with 2 inches (5 cm) of water. Bring to a boil over high heat. Turn the heat off and let stand for 15 minutes. Drain and run egg under cold water. Remove shells and chop.

2. Pour vinaigrette into jar, wiping down any splashes on the side of the jar. Layer cucumber, turkey, ham, lettuce, cheese and egg on top. Seal jar and refrigerate for up to 3 days.

3. When ready to serve, turn jar upside down in a bowl and let the dressing coat the salad.

Italian Salad

This salad reminds me of antipasti — cheese, salami, olives and peppers all rolled into one.

Tip

Banana peppers from a jar work best in this recipe. Make sure to squeeze out excess liquid; otherwise, it will water down the dressing.

● **1-quart (1 L) mason jar**

3 tbsp	Italian Vinaigrette (page 164)	45 mL
1	red bell pepper, sliced	1
2 tbsp	chopped drained hot banana peppers (see tip, at left)	30 mL
½ cup	halved cherry tomatoes	125 mL
1½ cups	roughly chopped escarole	375 mL
¼ cup	pitted black olives	60 mL
¼ cup	cubed Romano cheese	60 mL
4	slices soppressata salami, rolled	4

1. Pour vinaigrette into jar, wiping down any splashes on the side of the jar. Layer red pepper, banana peppers, tomatoes, escarole, olives, cheese and salami on top. Seal jar and refrigerate for up to 3 days.
2. When ready to serve, turn jar upside down in a bowl and let the dressing coat the salad.

Variation

Summery Italian Salad: Substitute about ½ cup (125 mL) cooled grilled bell pepper, zucchini or eggplant for the raw red pepper.

Roasted Potato, Sausage and Arugula Salad

This rustic Italian-inspired salad is particularly satisfying in the winter months.

MAKES
1 SERVING

Tips

You can roast just about any vegetable with this mixture. I try to keep it to just a few ingredients, so as not to overcomplicate the flavors, but up to ½ cup (125 mL) chopped fennel bulb, bell peppers or zucchini would be a nice addition.

You can also roast the sausage in a roasting pan in a 400°F (200°C) oven for 20 to 25 minutes. Turn the sausage after 10 minutes to create a golden color.

Caper berries are the fruit of the caper bush, while capers are the buds. Both are typically sold brined. Look for caper berries at well-stocked grocery or gourmet stores. If you can't find them, capers will work in their place.

- Preheat oven to 450°F (230°C)
- Rimmed baking sheet, lined with foil
- 1-quart (1 L) mason jar

5	small new potatoes (about 1 inch/2.5 cm in diameter), halved	5
½	red onion, sliced	½
1 cup	cherry tomatoes	250 mL
¼ cup	drained caper berries (see tip, at left), stemmed	60 mL
¼ cup	olive oil, divided	60 mL
2 tbsp	reduced balsamic vinegar (see tip, page 164), divided	30 mL
	Salt and freshly ground black pepper	
1	Italian sausage	1
1 cup	packed arugula	250 mL

1. In a medium bowl, toss together potatoes, onion, tomatoes, caper berries, half the oil and half the vinegar. Season with salt and pepper. Spread in a single layer on prepared baking sheet. Bake in preheated oven for 30 minutes or until a nice golden, caramelized crust forms. Let cool completely.

2. Meanwhile, preheat barbecue grill to high, with the fire on only one side of the grill. Place sausage over indirect heat (on the unlit side of the grill), cover and grill, turning often, for 15 minutes or until juices run clear. Let cool completely, then slice into rounds.

3. Pour the remaining oil and vinegar into jar, wiping down any splashes on the side of the jar. Layer roasted vegetables, sausage and arugula on top. Seal jar and refrigerate for up to 3 days.

4. When ready to serve, turn jar upside down in a bowl and let the dressing coat the salad.

Variation

Roasted Potato, Chicken and Arugula Salad: Substitute cold sliced grilled chicken for the sausage and skip step 2.

Asian Slaw with Honey Ginger Dressing

This delicious, crunchy slaw is full of fresh vegetables. The sweet honey ginger dressing is the perfect pairing for this light and airy dish. For a bit of a kick, try sprinkling a few hot pepper flakes on top.

Tips

Napa cabbage is an Asian vegetable that is lighter than traditional cabbage. It has a taste similar to celery and bok choy, and is ideal for salads and slaws.

For some extra heat, add 1 tsp (5 mL) finely chopped red chile peppers to the dressing.

- Preheat greased barbecue grill to high
- 1-quart (1 L) mason jar

1	boneless pork loin chop, about ¾-inch (2 cm) thick	1
1 tbsp	hoisin sauce	15 mL
1 tsp	grated gingerroot	5 mL
2 tbsp	sesame oil	30 mL
1 tbsp	seasoned rice vinegar	15 mL
1 tsp	liquid honey	5 mL
1 cup	julienned snap peas (see tip, page 36)	250 mL
1 cup	bean sprouts	250 mL
1 cup	julienned carrots	250 mL
½ cup	cooked edamame	125 mL
2 cups	shredded napa cabbage	500 mL
¼ cup	chopped green onions	60 mL
1 tsp	sesame seeds	5 mL

1. Brush both sides of pork chop with hoisin sauce. Place pork on prepared grill and grill for 1 to 2 minutes per side, turning once, or until browned on both sides. Reduce heat to medium and grill, turning occasionally, for 7 to 8 minutes or until just a hint of pink remains inside pork. Let cool completely, then cut into strips.

2. In a measuring cup, whisk together ginger, oil, vinegar and honey.

3. Pour dressing into jar, wiping down any splashes on the side of the jar. Layer snap peas, bean sprouts, carrots, edamame and cabbage on top, tightly packing the cabbage. Top with sliced pork, green onions and sesame seeds. Seal jar and refrigerate for up to 3 days.

4. When ready to serve, turn jar upside down in a bowl and let the dressing coat the salad.

Steakhouse Salad

This is my version of the classic iceberg wedge and blue cheese salad you get at steakhouses. The difference is, the steak is added to the salad instead of coming separately.

Tip

The radishes are what make this salad special. You can omit the cucumbers and double up on the radishes, or replace the cucumber with another crunchy vegetable, such as sliced fennel or celery.

- Preheat oven to 400°F (200°C)
- Rimmed baking sheet, with rack set on top
- 1-quart (1 L) mason jar

6 oz	boneless beef strip loin (New York strip) steak	175 mL
2 tbsp	olive oil, divided	30 mL
	Salt and freshly ground black pepper	
2 tbsp	Blue Cheese and Chive Dressing (page 170)	30 mL
½ cup	sliced radishes	125 mL
½ cup	sliced cucumber	125 mL
2 cups	sliced iceberg lettuce	500 mL
1 tbsp	chopped fresh chives	15 mL

1. Rub steak with 1 tbsp (15 mL) oil and season with salt and pepper. In a medium skillet, heat the remaining oil over high heat. Sear steak for 3 minutes per side and 1 minute per edge.

2. Transfer steak to rack over baking sheet. Roast in center of preheated oven for about 20 minutes for medium-rare, or to desired doneness. Remove from oven. Transfer to a cutting board and let rest for 5 to 10 minutes. Slice across the grain, then let cool completely.

3. Pour dressing into jar, wiping down any splashes on the side of the jar. Layer radishes, cucumber, lettuce, chives and steak on top. Seal jar and refrigerate for up to 3 days.

4. When ready to serve, turn jar upside down in a bowl and let the dressing coat the salad.

Variation

Meat Lovers Salad: Add 2 slices of bacon, cooked crisp, cooled and chopped, before the steak.

Hamburger in a Jar

After I made this salad for the first time, I was hooked. I've since passed it on to a few of my friends and they've turned it into a weeknight staple. It's sure to become one of your new favorites, too.

Tips

If you prefer, you can use chopped sweet pickles in this recipe.

For variety, swap out the Cheddar cheese for shredded mozzarella or Swiss cheese.

- 1-quart (1 L) mason jar
- 1-pint (500 mL) mason jar

1 tbsp	olive oil	15 mL
½ cup	finely chopped onion	125 mL
4 oz	lean ground beef	125 g
2 tbsp	Thousand Island Dressing (page 172)	30 mL
½ cup	chopped tomatoes	125 mL
¼ cup	chopped dill pickles	60 mL
2 cups	chopped iceberg lettuce	500 mL
¼ cup	chopped fresh dill	60 mL
¼ cup	shredded Cheddar cheese	60 mL

1. In a medium skillet, heat oil over medium-high heat. Add onion and cook, stirring occasionally, for 10 minutes or until golden. Using a slotted spoon, transfer onion to a bowl.

2. Add beef to the pan and cook, breaking beef up with a spoon, for 7 to 10 minutes or until no longer pink. Drain off fat, then add beef to onion, stirring to combine. Let cool completely.

3. Spoon dressing into the 1-quart (1 L) jar, wiping down any splashes on the side of the jar. Layer tomatoes, pickles, lettuce, dill and cheese on top. Seal jar and refrigerate for up to 3 days.

4. Place beef mixture in the 1-pint (500 mL) jar. Seal jar and refrigerate for up to 3 days.

5. When ready to serve, remove lid from beef mixture and microwave on High for 40 seconds or until warm. Turn salad jar upside down in a bowl and let the dressing coat the salad. Top with warm beef.

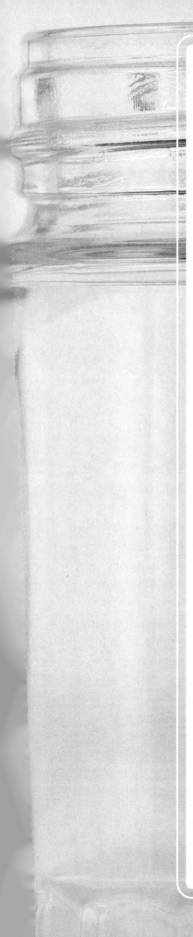

Rice Bowls

Mediterranean Rice Bowl

Think of this dish as a Greek salad with rice. It's simple but delicious.

Tip

Drizzling olive oil on hummus makes it less thick and brings out the flavor in the dip.

- 1-quart (1 L) mason jar

1 cup	water	250 mL
½ cup	long-grain white rice	125 mL
¼ tsp	salt	1 mL
¼ cup	hummus	60 mL
1 tbsp	extra virgin olive oil	15 mL
½ cup	halved cherry tomatoes	125 mL
¼ cup	chopped cucumber	60 mL
¼ cup	roughly chopped roasted red bell pepper (see tip, page 115)	60 mL
2 tbsp	finely chopped red onion	30 mL
¼ cup	roughly chopped pitted kalamata olives	60 mL
½ cup	mesclun	125 mL
¼ cup	crumbled feta cheese	60 mL

1. In a medium saucepan, bring water to a boil over high heat. Stir in rice and salt, reduce heat to low, cover and simmer for 20 minutes or until rice is tender and water is absorbed. Remove from heat and fluff with a fork. Let cool completely.

2. Spoon hummus into jar and drizzle with oil, wiping down any splashes on the side of the jar. Layer rice, tomatoes, cucumber, roasted pepper, onion, olives, mesclun and feta on top. Seal jar and refrigerate for up to 3 days.

3. Remove jar from the refrigerator 30 minutes before serving, to bring it to room temperature. Turn jar upside down in a bowl, scooping out the hummus and dolloping it over the rice.

Variation

Mediterranean Chicken Rice Bowl: Add ½ cup (125 mL) cold chopped grilled chicken on top of the mesclun.

Santa Fe Rice Bowl

There's something comforting about a bowl of rice topped with veggies and cheese. Simply put, it's the perfect one-dish meal.

MAKES
1 SERVING

Tips

The package directions for most brown rice specify a longer cooking time, usually between 40 and 55 minutes, but I like to start checking for doneness at 30 minutes, to make sure it doesn't get mushy.

For crisper cilantro, cut out a small circle of parchment paper and place it on top of the cheese, then place the cilantro on top.

- 1-quart (1 L) mason jar

1¼ cups	water	300 mL
½ cup	long-grain brown rice	125 mL
¼ tsp	salt	1 mL
½ cup	chopped avocado	125 mL
1 tsp	freshly squeezed lemon juice	5 mL
1 tbsp	sour cream	15 mL
1 tsp	hot pepper sauce	5 mL
½ cup	rinsed drained canned black beans	125 mL
½ cup	sliced cherry tomatoes	125 mL
¼ cup	chopped orange bell pepper	60 mL
¼ cup	shredded Cheddar cheese	60 mL
1 tbsp	chopped fresh cilantro	15 mL

1. In a medium saucepan, bring water to a boil over high heat. Stir in rice and salt, reduce heat to low, cover and simmer for 30 to 50 minutes (see tip, at left) or until rice is tender and water is absorbed. Remove from heat and fluff with a fork. Let cool completely.

2. Place avocado in a bowl and drizzle with lemon juice, tossing to coat.

3. Spoon sour cream into jar and drizzle with hot pepper sauce, wiping down any splashes on the side of the jar. Layer rice, beans, tomatoes, avocado, orange pepper, cheese and cilantro. Seal jar and refrigerate for up to 3 days.

4. Remove jar from the refrigerator 30 minutes before serving, to bring it to room temperature. Turn jar upside down in a bowl, scooping out the sour cream and dolloping it over the rice.

Variation

Chicken Santa Fe Rice Bowl: Add 1 cup (250 mL) cold chopped cooked chicken on top of the orange pepper.

Spicy Tofu and Vegetable Rice Bowl

I'm not a vegetarian, but I'd consider it after eating this bowl. It satisfies me on every level. The spicy tofu combines with the crisp, fresh vegetables and comforting rice for a truly special meal.

MAKES 1 SERVING

Tips

The easiest way to grate the cucumber and carrots is to use the coarse side of a box grater.

To "julienne" means to cut into matchstick-shaped pieces.

For an added punch of flavor, toss the vegetables with 1 tbsp (15 mL) seasoned rice vinegar before adding them to the jar. This will also cut the spiciness of the tofu.

- 1-quart (1 L) mason jar

2 tbsp	hot pepper sauce, divided	30 mL
1 tbsp	Asian sweet chile sauce	15 mL
1 tbsp	sesame oil	15 mL
1 tbsp	water	15 mL
½ cup	cubed firm tofu	125 mL
1 cup	water	250 mL
½ cup	long-grain white rice	125 mL
¼ tsp	salt	1 mL
1 tbsp	canola oil	15 mL
½ cup	grated cucumber (see tip, at left)	125 mL
½ cup	grated carrots	125 mL
½ cup	julienned radishes (see tip, at left)	125 mL
½ cup	julienned snap peas	125 mL
¼ cup	chopped fresh mint	60 mL
¼ cup	chopped fresh cilantro	60 mL
1 tsp	sesame seeds	5 mL

1. In a small bowl, combine 1 tbsp (5 mL) hot pepper sauce, chile sauce, sesame oil and 1 tbsp (15 mL) water. Add tofu and toss to coat. Cover and refrigerate for at least 1 hour or up to 4 hours.

2. Meanwhile, in a medium saucepan, bring 1 cup (250 mL) water to a boil over high heat. Stir in rice and salt, reduce heat to low, cover and simmer for 20 minutes or until rice is tender and water is absorbed. Remove from heat and fluff with a fork. Let cool completely.

Tips

If you would prefer to eat this rice bowl warm, there's no need to let it warm to room temperature for 30 minutes. Instead, simply remove the lid and microwave the jar on High for 1 minute.

3. In a medium saucepan, heat canola oil over high heat. Remove tofu from marinade, discarding marinade, and add tofu to the pan. Sear, turning once, for 1 minute per side. Reduce heat to medium-low and cook, stirring occasionally, for 5 to 10 minutes or until crispy and brown on all sides. Transfer tofu to a plate lined with paper towels and let cool completely.

4. Layer rice, tofu, cucumber, carrots, radishes, snap peas, mint, cilantro and sesame seeds in jar. Drizzle the remaining hot pepper sauce on top. Seal jar and refrigerate for up to 3 days.

5. Remove jar from the refrigerator 30 minutes before serving, to bring it to room temperature (see tip, at left). Turn jar upside down in a bowl.

Fried Egg Rice Bowl

This is a simplified version of bibimbap, a Korean dish often made of rice, vegetables and a fried egg. When you make it fresh, the runny egg acts as a sauce for the rice, but it's just as good cold or at room temperature.

Tip

The package directions for most brown rice specify a longer cooking time, usually between 40 and 55 minutes, but I like to start checking for doneness at 30 minutes, to make sure it doesn't get mushy.

- 1-quart (1 L) mason jar

1¼ cups	water	300 mL
½ cup	long-grain brown rice	125 mL
¼ tsp	salt	1 mL
1 tsp	butter	5 mL
2	large eggs	2
1 tsp	finely chopped garlic	5 mL
½ tsp	packed brown sugar	2 mL
1 tbsp	sesame oil	15 mL
1 tsp	hot pepper sauce	5 mL
1 tsp	unseasoned rice vinegar	5 mL
1 tsp	water	5 mL
¼ cup	chopped avocado	60 mL
½ tsp	freshly squeezed lemon juice	2 mL
¼ cup	chopped green onions	60 mL
¼ cup	chopped carrots	60 mL
1 tbsp	chopped fresh flat-leaf (Italian) parsley	15 mL

1. In a medium saucepan, bring water to a boil over high heat. Stir in rice and salt, reduce heat to low, cover and simmer for 30 to 50 minutes (see tip, at left) or until rice is tender and water is absorbed. Remove from heat and fluff with a fork. Let cool completely.

2. In a medium nonstick skillet, melt butter over medium heat, swirling to evenly coat the pan. Heat until butter begins to sizzle. Crack eggs into opposite sides of the pan and cook for 2 minutes without moving the eggs. Flip eggs over and cook for 1 minute or until yolks are firm. Let cool completely.

3. In a measuring cup, whisk together garlic, brown sugar, sesame oil, hot pepper sauce, vinegar and 1 tsp (5 mL) water.

4. Place avocado in a bowl and drizzle with lemon juice, tossing to coat.

Tip

When ready to serve, you can transfer the eggs to a microwave-safe plate and pierce the yolks with a fork to make sure they don't explode while cooking. Microwave them on High for 30 seconds or until warm.

5. Pour dressing into jar, wiping down any splashes on the side of the jar. Layer rice, green onions, carrots, avocado and parsley on top. Place a parchment paper round on top of the parsley and top with eggs. Seal jar and refrigerate for up to 2 days.

6. Remove jar from the refrigerator 30 minutes before serving, to bring it to room temperature. Remove eggs and parchment paper, turn jar upside down in a bowl and let the dressing coat the rice. Top with eggs.

Variation

Bacon and Egg Rice Bowl: Add 2 slices of Canadian or regular bacon, cooked, chopped and cooled, on top of the avocado.

Tofu, Snow Pea and Cabbage Rice Bowl

When I'm in a vegetarian mood, this dish is completely satisfying. It's crunchy, comforting and healthy.

Tips

The package directions for most brown rice specify a longer cooking time, usually between 40 and 55 minutes, but I like to start checking for doneness at 30 minutes, to make sure it doesn't get mushy.

If you would prefer to make this up to 3 days ahead, use 1 tbsp (15 mL) of the dressing to coat the tofu before adding it to the salad. This will prevent the tofu from becoming too rubbery during the longer storage.

- 1-quart (1 L) mason jar

1¼ cups	water	300 mL
½ cup	long-grain brown rice	125 mL
¼ tsp	salt	1 mL
3 tbsp	Sesame Dressing (page 167)	45 mL
½ cup	sliced snow peas	125 mL
½ cup	sliced carrots	125 mL
1 cup	sliced napa cabbage	250 mL
1 cup	cubed firm tofu	250 mL

1. In a medium saucepan, bring water to a boil over high heat. Stir in rice and salt, reduce heat to low, cover and simmer for 30 to 50 minutes (see tip, at left) or until rice is tender and water is absorbed. Remove from heat and fluff with a fork. Let cool completely.

2. Pour dressing into jar, wiping down any splashes on the side of the jar. Layer rice, snow peas, carrots, cabbage and tofu on top. Seal jar and refrigerate for up to 1 day (see tip, at left).

3. Remove jar from the refrigerator 30 minutes before serving, to bring it to room temperature. Turn jar upside down in a bowl and let the dressing coat the rice.

Roasted Salmon, Bok Choy and Mushroom Rice Bowl

Salmon is easy to cook and can be enjoyed hot or cold, so it's a perfect protein to pack for lunch. This is a simple rice bowl. You can add more flavors or vegetables, but sometimes simple is best.

MAKES 1 SERVING

Tips

To remove the shiitake mushroom stems, pull on them gently. They should pop right off. Save them for making soup stock or discard.

If you would prefer to eat this rice bowl warm, there's no need to let it warm to room temperature for 30 minutes. Instead, simply remove the lid and microwave the jar on High in 20-second intervals for up to 1 minute. Be careful not to overheat it, as the salmon will become rubbery and the rice will get hard.

Variation

Tofu Rice Bowl: Omit the salmon, pepper and ¼ tsp (1 mL) of the salt, and skip step 2. Toss 1 cup (250 mL) cubed firm tofu with 1 tsp (2 mL) of the soy sauce and add on top of the mushroom mixture.

- Preheat oven to 450°F (230°C)
- Rimmed baking sheet, lined with foil
- 1-quart (1 L) mason jar

1 cup	water	250 mL
½ cup	long-grain white rice	125 mL
½ tsp	salt, divided	2 mL
3 oz	skin-on salmon fillet	90 g
¼ tsp	freshly ground black pepper	1 mL
2 tbsp	olive oil	30 mL
1 cup	chopped shiitake mushroom caps	250 mL
1½ cups	chopped bok choy	375 mL
2 tbsp	soy sauce	30 mL

1. In a medium saucepan, bring water to a boil over high heat. Stir in rice and ¼ tsp (1 mL) salt, reduce heat to low, cover and simmer for 20 minutes or until rice is tender and water is absorbed. Remove from heat and fluff with a fork. Let cool completely.

2. Meanwhile, place salmon, skin side down, on prepared baking sheet and season with pepper and the remaining salt. Roast in preheated oven for 12 to 15 minutes or until fish is opaque and flakes easily when tested with a fork. Flake salmon into pieces, discarding skin if desired, then let cool completely.

3. Meanwhile, in a medium skillet, heat oil over medium-high heat. Add mushrooms and cook, stirring, for 3 to 4 minutes or until starting to brown. Add bok choy and cook, stirring, for 1 to 2 minutes or until slightly wilted. Let cool completely.

4. Pour soy sauce into jar, wiping down any splashes on the side of the jar. Layer rice, mushroom mixture and salmon on top. Seal jar and refrigerate for up to 3 days.

5. Remove jar from the refrigerator 30 minutes before serving, to bring it to room temperature (see tip, at left). Turn jar upside down in a bowl and let the soy sauce coat the rice.

California Roll Bowl

This is exactly what you think it is: a deconstructed California roll. All the things you love about your favorite sushi snack are stuffed into a jar.

Tip

If you can't find sushi rice, long-grain white rice will do. The cooking time is the same.

- 1-quart (1 L) mason jar

½ cup	sushi rice	125 mL
1 cup	water	250 mL
1 tbsp	soy sauce	15 mL
1 tbsp	unseasoned rice vinegar	15 mL
1 tbsp	sesame oil	15 mL
½ cup	chopped avocado	125 mL
1 tsp	freshly squeezed lemon juice	5 mL
2 tbsp	drained pickled ginger	30 mL
1 cup	chopped cucumber	250 mL
½ cup	thawed frozen chopped cooked crabmeat or imitation crabmeat	125 mL
1 tbsp	sesame seeds	15 mL

1. In a colander, rinse sushi rice under cold water until water runs clear. In a medium saucepan, bring water to a boil over high heat. Stir in rice, reduce heat to low, cover and simmer for 20 minutes or until rice is tender and water is absorbed. Remove from heat and fluff with a fork. Let cool completely.

2. In a measuring cup, whisk together soy sauce, vinegar and sesame oil.

3. Place avocado in a bowl and drizzle with lemon juice, tossing to coat.

4. Pour dressing into jar, wiping down any splashes on the side of the jar. Layer ginger, cucumber, rice, crab and avocado on top. Sprinkle with sesame seeds. Seal jar and refrigerate for up to 3 days.

5. Remove jar from the refrigerator 30 minutes before serving, to bring it to room temperature. Turn jar upside down into a bowl and let the dressing coat the rice.

Variation

Spicy Crab California Rice Bowl: Toss the crabmeat with 1 tbsp (15 mL) mayonnaise and ½ tsp (2 mL) prepared wasabi before adding it to the jar.

Shrimp, Orange and Avocado Bowl

There are certain food combinations that work so well together you wonder why they are ever served on their own. Shrimp, oranges and avocados is one of those trios.

Tip

You could slice the oranges into rounds instead of sectioning them, but that would require you to use a knife when eating the rice bowl, which can be awkward.

- 1-quart (1 L) mason jar

1 cup	water	250 mL
½ cup	long-grain white rice	125 mL
¼ tsp	salt	1 mL
½ cup	chopped avocado	125 mL
1 tsp	freshly squeezed lemon juice	5 mL
3 tbsp	Citrus Vinaigrette (page 166)	45 mL
1 cup	thawed frozen cooked shrimp	250 mL
1 cup	sectioned oranges (pith removed)	250 mL
¼ cup	chopped fresh cilantro	60 mL

1. In a medium saucepan, bring water to a boil over high heat. Stir in rice and salt, reduce heat to low, cover and simmer for 20 minutes or until rice is tender and water is absorbed. Remove from heat and fluff with a fork. Let cool completely.

2. Place avocado in a bowl and drizzle with lemon juice, tossing to coat.

3. Pour vinaigrette into jar, wiping down any splashes on the side of the jar. Layer rice, shrimp, oranges, avocado and cilantro on top. Seal jar and refrigerate for up to 3 days.

4. Remove jar from the refrigerator 30 minutes before serving, to bring it to room temperature. Turn jar upside down in a bowl and let the dressing coat the rice.

Variation

Chicken, Orange and Avocado Bowl: Substitute 1 cup (250 mL) cold chopped cooked chicken for the shrimp.

Cobb Rice Bowl

This is a variation of a Cobb salad in rice bowl form. It's impossible to get tired of the flavors.

Tips

Adding a little lemon juice to the guacamole prevents it from getting brown.

Cooked meat, such as the chicken in this recipe, should be eaten within 3 days of when it is cooked. Make sure the chicken's total storage time does not exceed 3 days.

- 1-quart (1 L) mason jar

1 cup	water	250 mL
$\frac{1}{2}$ cup	long-grain white rice	125 mL
$\frac{1}{4}$ tsp	salt	1 mL
$\frac{1}{4}$ cup	guacamole	60 mL
1 tsp	freshly squeezed lemon juice	5 mL
$\frac{1}{4}$ cup	chopped roasted red bell pepper (see tip, page 115)	60 mL
$\frac{1}{2}$ cup	halved cherry tomatoes	125 mL
$\frac{1}{2}$ cup	cold chopped rotisserie chicken	125 mL
$\frac{1}{4}$ cup	crumbled blue cheese	60 mL

1. In a medium saucepan, bring water to a boil over high heat. Stir in rice and salt, reduce heat to low, cover and simmer for 20 minutes or until rice is tender and water is absorbed. Remove from heat and fluff with a fork. Let cool completely.

2. In a small bowl, combine guacamole and lemon juice.

3. Spoon guacamole mixture into jar, wiping down any splashes on the side of the jar. Layer rice, roasted pepper, tomatoes, chicken and blue cheese on top. Seal jar and refrigerate for up to 3 days.

4. Remove jar from the refrigerator 30 minutes before serving, to bring it to room temperature. Turn jar upside down in a bowl, scooping out the guacamole and dolloping it over the rice.

Variation

Cobb Brown Rice Bowl: Substitute $\frac{1}{2}$ cup (125 mL) long-grain brown rice for the white rice and add 10 to 30 minutes to the cooking time (see tip, page 135).

Chicken, Avocado and Mango Rice Bowl

This rice bowl has only a few ingredients, but it's full of flavor. The citrus vinaigrette adds a refreshing note and turns it into a delicious cold lunch.

Tips

Never buy mangos that are completely green — they likely will never ripen. Look for mangos that have a bit of give when squeezed and a touch of reddish-orange color.

Cooked meat, such as the chicken in this recipe, should be eaten within 3 days of when it is cooked. Make sure the chicken's total storage time does not exceed 3 days.

The package directions for most brown rice specify a longer cooking time, usually between 40 and 55 minutes, but I like to start checking for doneness at 30 minutes, to make sure it doesn't get mushy.

- 1-quart (1 L) mason jar

1¼ cups	water	300 mL
½ cup	long-grain brown rice	125 mL
¼ tsp	salt	1 mL
1 cup	cubed mango	250 mL
½ cup	cubed avocado	125 mL
2 tbsp	Citrus Vinaigrette (page 166), divided	30 mL
1 cup	cold shredded rotisserie chicken	250 mL

1. In a medium saucepan, bring water to a boil over high heat. Stir in rice and salt, reduce heat to low, cover and simmer for 30 to 50 minutes (see tip, at left) or until rice is tender and water is absorbed. Remove from heat and fluff with a fork. Let cool completely.

2. Place mango and avocado in a bowl and drizzle with 1 tbsp (15 mL) vinaigrette, tossing to coat.

3. Pour the remaining vinaigrette into jar, wiping down any splashes on the side of the jar. Layer rice, chicken and mango mixture on top. Seal jar and refrigerate for up to 3 days.

4. Remove jar from the refrigerator 30 minutes before serving, to bring it to room temperature. Turn jar upside down in a bowl and let the dressing coat the rice.

Souvlaki Dinner Bowl

If you've ever ordered a souvlaki dinner from a Greek restaurant, you'll immediately understand how easily it translates into bowl form. I've omitted the potatoes, but otherwise the result is pretty much the same.

**MAKES
1 SERVING**

Tips

If you don't have a grill, you can pan-fry the chicken. Season the chicken with salt and pepper. In a medium skillet, heat 1 tsp (5 mL) olive oil over medium-high heat. Add chicken and cook for 5 to 6 minutes per side, turning once, until no longer pink inside. Transfer to a cutting board and let cool completely, then slice.

When ready to serve, you can transfer the chicken to a microwave-safe plate first and microwave it on High for 1 minute or until warm. Then add it to the top of the rice bowl.

Variation

Pork Souvlaki Dinner: Substitute 1 cup (250 mL) cold sliced grilled pork for the chicken, reduce the salt to ¼ tsp (1 mL), omit the oil and pepper, and skip step 2.

- Preheat barbecue grill to medium-high (see tip, at left)
- 1-quart (1 L) mason jar

1 cup	water	250 mL
½ cup	long-grain white rice	125 mL
½ tsp	salt, divided	2 mL
1	boneless skinless chicken breast (about 4 oz/125 g)	1
1 tsp	olive oil	5 mL
¼ tsp	freshly ground black pepper	1 mL
¼ cup	tzatziki	60 mL
½ cup	chopped cucumber	125 mL
½ cup	quartered cherry tomatoes	125 mL
2	lemon wedges	2

1. In a medium saucepan, bring water to a boil over high heat. Stir in rice and ¼ tsp (1 mL) salt, reduce heat to low, cover and simmer for 20 minutes or until rice is tender and water is absorbed. Remove from heat and fluff with a fork. Let cool completely.

2. Meanwhile, brush chicken with oil and season with pepper and the remaining salt. Place on preheated grill and grill for 5 to 6 minutes per side, turning once, until chicken is no longer pink inside. Transfer to a cutting board and let cool completely, then slice.

3. Spoon tzatziki into jar, wiping down any splashes on the side of the jar. Layer rice, cucumber, tomatoes, chicken and lemon wedges on top. Seal jar and refrigerate for up to 3 days.

4. Remove jar from the refrigerator 30 minutes before serving, to bring it to room temperature. Remove the lemon wedges and turn jar upside down in a bowl, scooping out the tzatziki and dolloping it over the rice. Squeeze the juice from the lemon wedges over top.

Teriyaki Rice Bowl

This is a classic. No need to say more.

Tips

The chicken can be roasted instead of grilled. Preheat the oven to 400°F (200°C). Place the chicken on a rimmed baking sheet lined with foil, brush with oil and season with pepper. Roast for 25 minutes, turning once, until chicken is no longer pink inside.

If you don't have teriyaki sauce on hand, combine 1 tsp (5 mL) packed brown sugar, 1 tbsp (15 mL) soy sauce and 1 tbsp (15 mL) unseasoned rice vinegar. It's not exactly the same, but it's a good backup.

Use caution when removing the jar from the microwave, as the contents could be quite hot.

- Preheat barbecue grill to high (see tip, at left)
- 1-quart (1 L) mason jar

1¼ cups	water	300 mL
½ cup	long-grain brown rice	125 mL
¼ tsp	salt	1 mL
1	boneless skinless chicken breast (about 4 oz/125 g)	1
1 tsp	olive oil	5 mL
¼ tsp	freshly ground black pepper	1 mL
3 tbsp	teriyaki sauce	45 mL
½ cup	cooked edamame	125 mL
½ cup	finely chopped carrots	125 mL
¼ cup	chopped green onions	60 mL

1. In a medium saucepan, bring water to a boil over high heat. Stir in rice and salt, reduce heat to low, cover and simmer for 30 to 50 minutes (see tip, page 135) or until rice is tender and water is absorbed. Remove from heat and fluff with a fork. Let cool completely.

2. Meanwhile, brush chicken with oil and season with pepper. Place on preheated grill and grill for 5 to 6 minutes per side, turning once, until chicken is no longer pink inside. Transfer to a cutting board and let cool completely, then slice.

3. Pour teriyaki sauce into jar, wiping down any splashes on the side of the jar. Layer rice, edamame, carrots, chicken and green onions on top. Seal jar and refrigerate for up to 3 days.

4. When ready to serve, remove lid and microwave on High for 1 to 2 minutes or until heated through. Turn jar upside down in a bowl and let the teriyaki sauce coat the rice.

Variation

Teriyaki Tofu: Substitute 1 cup (250 mL) cubed firm tofu for the chicken, omit the oil and pepper, and skip step 2. Refrigerate for up to 1 day.

Pork Burrito Bowl

The pairings of pork and barbecue sauce and rice and beans make this rice bowl a homerun.

**MAKES
1 SERVING**

Tips

The package directions for most brown rice specify a longer cooking time, usually between 40 and 55 minutes, but I like to start checking for doneness at 30 minutes, to make sure it doesn't get mushy.

If you find this dish too saucy, omit the barbecue sauce and layer the beans on the bottom of the jar; the sauce on the beans will flavor the rice bowl.

Use caution when removing the jar from the microwave, as the contents could be quite hot.

- Preheat greased barbecue grill to high
- 1-quart (1 L) mason jar

1¼ cups	water	300 mL
½ cup	long-grain brown rice	125 mL
	Salt	
1	boneless pork loin chop, about ¾-inch (2 cm) thick	1
1 tbsp	olive oil	15 mL
	Freshly ground black pepper	
2 tbsp	barbecue sauce	30 mL
½ cup	canned barbecue baked beans	125 mL
¼ cup	chopped red onion	60 mL
1 cup	shredded purple cabbage	250 mL

1. In a medium saucepan, bring water to a boil over high heat. Stir in rice and ¼ tsp (1 mL) salt, reduce heat to low, cover and simmer for 30 to 50 minutes (see tip, at left) or until rice is tender and water is absorbed. Remove from heat and fluff with a fork. Let cool completely.

2. Brush both sides of pork chop with oil and season with salt and pepper. Place pork on prepared grill and grill for 1 to 2 minutes per side, turning once, or until browned on both sides. Reduce heat to medium and grill, turning occasionally, for 7 to 8 minutes or until just a hint of pink remains inside pork. Let cool completely, then cut into strips.

3. Pour barbecue sauce into jar, wiping down any splashes on the side of the jar. Layer rice, beans, onion, cabbage and pork on top. Seal jar and refrigerate for up to 3 days.

4. When ready to serve, remove lid and microwave on High for 1 to 2 minutes or until heated through. Turn jar upside down in a bowl and let the barbecue sauce coat the rice.

Variation

Chicken Burrito Bowl: Substitute 1 cup (250 mL) cold cooked chopped chicken for the pork and skip step 2.

Cabbage Roll Bowl

My great-aunt, Stella Mazur, made delicious cabbage rolls. She claimed the secret was chopped fresh dill and a simple, tangy tomato sauce. When developing ideas for this book, I realized that a cabbage roll could translate into a rice bowl. And it does. Thank you, Aunt Stella!

Tip

If you would prefer to eat this rice bowl warm, there's no need to let it warm to room temperature for 30 minutes. Instead, simply remove the lid and microwave the jar on High for 1 minute. It is best served warm rather than piping hot. Use caution when removing the jar from the microwave.

- 1-quart (1 L) mason jar

1 cup	water	250 mL
½ cup	long-grain white rice	125 mL
½ tsp	salt, divided	2 mL
4 oz	lean ground beef	125 g
¼ cup	tomato sauce	60 mL
¼ cup	finely chopped onion	60 mL
½ cup	finely chopped napa cabbage	125 mL
¼ cup	finely chopped fresh dill	60 mL
¼ cup	finely chopped fresh flat-leaf (Italian) parsley	60 mL
2 tbsp	pine nuts	30 mL

1. In a medium saucepan, bring water to a boil over high heat. Stir in rice and ¼ tsp (1 mL) salt, reduce heat to low, cover and simmer for 20 minutes or until rice is tender and water is absorbed. Remove from heat and fluff with a fork. Let cool completely.

2. In a nonstick skillet, over medium-high heat, cook beef and the remaining salt, breaking beef up with a spoon, for 8 to 10 minutes or until no longer pink. Using a slotted spoon, transfer beef to a plate lined with paper towels and let cool completely.

3. Pour tomato sauce into jar, wiping down any splashes on the side of the jar. Layer rice, onion, cabbage, beef, dill, parsley and pine nuts on top. Seal jar and refrigerate for up to 3 days.

4. Remove jar from the refrigerator 30 minutes before serving, to bring it to room temperature (see tip, at left). Turn jar upside down in a bowl and let the tomato sauce coat the rice.

Hearty Meals

Lasagna in a Jar

This is a great portable meal to take with you for a hearty lunch or dinner. The recipe is vegetarian, but it's easy to make a meat version instead (see variation).

Tips

Use a rasp grater, such as Microplane, to grate the Parmesan cheese. It will make feathery shreds that create a more delicate crisp once baked.

If you're short on time, skip baking the Parmesan chips in step 1 and just sprinkle the Parmesan on top of the mozzarella layers.

- Preheat oven to 400°F (200°C)
- Rimmed baking sheet, lined with parchment paper
- Two 1-pint (500 mL) wide-mouth mason jars

¼ cup	freshly grated Parmesan cheese (see tip, at left)	60 mL
½ cup	finely chopped trimmed spinach leaves	125 mL
1 tsp	finely chopped garlic	5 mL
1 tsp	salt	5 mL
1 tsp	freshly ground black pepper	5 mL
1 cup	ricotta cheese	250 mL
1 tbsp	olive oil	15 mL
1½ cups	tomato sauce	375 mL
6	cooked lasagna noodles, broken into smaller pieces	6
¾ cup	shredded mozzarella cheese	175 mL

1. Spread Parmesan in two piles, spaced at least 4 inches (10 cm) apart, on prepared baking sheet. Spread each into a thin circle about 2 inches (5 cm) in diameter. Bake in preheated oven for 6 to 8 minutes or until cheese is golden and crisp. Gently slide a spatula under each chip to loosen, then let cool completely on pan on a wire rack.

2. Meanwhile, in a small bowl, combine spinach, garlic, salt, pepper, ricotta and oil.

3. Spoon ¼ cup (60 mL) tomato sauce into each jar. Add one-quarter of the noodle pieces, then top with half of the ricotta mixture, pressing down gently as you layer. Add another quarter of the noodle pieces, then add ¼ cup (60 mL) sauce and sprinkle with half the mozzarella. Add another layer of noodles, ½ cup (125 mL) sauce and the remaining ricotta mixture. Top with the remaining noodles, then the remaining sauce and mozzarella. Place a parchment paper round on top of each, then top with a Parmesan chip. Seal jars and refrigerate for up to 3 days.

Tips

Use caution when removing the jar from the microwave, as the glass could be quite hot.

If you want to serve two people at the same time, you can microwave both jars together, but increase the time by 30 seconds.

4. When ready to serve, remove lid and lift out parchment paper and Parmesan chip. Microwave jar on High for 2 minutes or until warmed through and mozzarella is melted. Replace Parmesan chip and serve.

Variation

Meat Lover's Lasagna: Use a Bolognese sauce (such as the one on page 158) instead of tomato sauce. Be sure to chill the sauce before assembling the lasagna in the jar.

Layered Eggplant Dinner

You don't have to be a vegetarian to enjoy this dinner. I like to top mine with some arugula after it's warmed up.

Tips

You will have to fold the eggplant slices to fit them into the mason jars.

Ten thin crosswise slices of zucchini will work just as well in this recipe. Or try alternating zucchini slices and eggplant slices.

Use caution when removing the jar from the microwave, as the glass could be quite hot.

If you want to serve two people at the same time, you can microwave both jars together, but increase the time by 30 seconds.

- Two 1-pint (500 mL) wide-mouth mason jars

8	thin crosswise slices eggplant	8
1 tbsp	salt	15 mL
1	large egg	1
1 cup	extra-fine dry bread crumbs or panko (Japanese bread crumbs)	250 mL
1/4 cup	vegetable oil	60 mL
1 cup	tomato sauce	250 mL
1/2 cup	shredded mozzarella cheese	125 mL
6	basil leaves, left whole or chopped	6

1. Place eggplant slices on a cutting board and season both sides with salt. Let stand for 30 to 60 minutes or until water beads on top of eggplant. Rinse under cold running water and pat dry.

2. In a small bowl, whisk egg. Spread bread crumbs on a plate. Dip eggplant slices in egg, shaking off excess, then coat in bread crumbs, shaking off excess. Discard excess egg and bread crumbs.

3. In a medium skillet, heat oil over medium-high heat. Add eggplant and fry for 2 to 3 minutes per side or until golden brown. Let cool completely.

4. Layer tomato sauce, folded eggplant slices, mozzarella and basil in jars, dividing evenly. Seal jars and refrigerate for up to 3 days.

5. When ready to serve, remove lid and microwave on High for 1 minute or until warmed through.

Variation

Meat Lovers Eggplant: Substitute 1/2 cup (125 mL) tomato sauce with Bolognese sauce.

Classic Cobb Salad (page 114) and Shrimp Cocktail Salad (page 110)

Asian Slaw with Honey Ginger Dressing (page 119)

Santa Fe Rice Bowl (page 125)

Souvlaki Dinner Bowl (page 136)

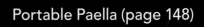
Portable Paella (page 148)

Shepherd's Pie with Lamb and Wilted Spinach (page 160)

Basic Vinaigrette (page 164)

Avocado Lime Dressing (page 170) & Ranch Dressing (page 171)

Cute and Clever Key Lime Pie (page 176)

No-Bake Raspberry Tarts (page 177)

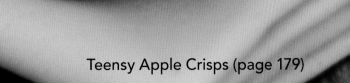
Teensy Apple Crisps (page 179)

Mike's Famous Tomato and Lentil Soup-Stew

Mike is my husband, and this is his soup-stew. He makes a huge batch on the weekend and takes it for lunch for a solid week. Some think it is a soup. Others call it a stew. Whatever you call it, it's hearty and healthy, and it's a meal worthy of lunch or dinner.

MAKES 6 SERVINGS

Tips

You can easily substitute cooked dried lentils for the canned lentils. You'll need to cook 2 cups (500 mL) dried lentils to get 4½ cups (1.125 L) cooked.

Use caution when removing the jar from the microwave, as the glass could be quite hot.

If serving two people at the same time, you can microwave two jars together, but increase the time by 1 minute. Do not microwave more than two jars simultaneously.

- Six 1-pint (500 mL) wide-mouth mason jars

2 tbsp	olive oil	30 mL
3	cloves garlic, minced	3
1	jalapeño pepper, seeded and chopped	1
1 cup	chopped fresh flat-leaf (Italian) parsley	250 mL
4½ cups	canned whole tomatoes, with juice	1.125 L
3½ cups	canned crushed tomatoes	875 mL
4½ cups	rinsed drained canned lentils	1.125 L
1 tbsp	dried oregano	15 mL
1 tbsp	freshly ground black pepper	15 mL
1 tsp	salt	5 mL
1 cup	water	250 mL
2 tbsp	chopped fresh basil	30 mL

1. In a large pot, heat oil over medium-high heat. Add garlic, jalapeño and parsley; cook, stirring, for 1 minute. Add whole tomatoes, crushing them with the back of a spoon. Stir in crushed tomatoes, lentils, oregano, pepper, salt and water; bring to a boil. Reduce heat and simmer, stirring occasionally, for 1 hour to blend the flavors. Let cool completely.

2. Divide soup evenly among jars and top with basil. Seal jars and refrigerate for up to 4 days.

3. When ready to serve, remove lid and microwave on High for 3 minutes or until warmed through.

Variation

Chicken, Tomato and Lentil Soup: Cook 3 boneless skinless chicken breasts, shred and let cool completely. Divide chicken evenly among the jars.

Moroccan Squash and Chickpea Stew

This is a "throw it all into one pot" kind of stew. It's flavored with Moroccan spices and works well with a dollop of sour cream to finish it off.

Tips

When ready to eat, add a dollop of sour cream to the hot soup for extra creaminess.

Use caution when removing the jar from the microwave, as the glass could be quite hot.

If serving two people at the same time, you can microwave two jars together, but increase the time by 30 seconds. Do not microwave more than two jars simultaneously.

- Four 1-quart (1 L) wide-mouth mason jars

1 tbsp	olive oil	15 mL
3	cloves garlic, finely chopped	3
1	small onion, chopped	1
1 tbsp	ground cumin	15 mL
1 tbsp	ground cinnamon	15 mL
1 tsp	hot pepper flakes	5 mL
2 cups	chopped butternut squash	500 mL
2 cups	rinsed drained canned chickpeas	500 mL
1 cup	rinsed drained canned lentils	250 mL
1 cup	canned diced tomatoes, with juice	250 mL
3 cups	ready-to-use vegetable broth	750 mL
1 tsp	salt	5 mL
1 tsp	freshly ground black pepper	5 mL
2 tbsp	chopped fresh basil	30 mL

1. In a large pot, heat oil over medium-high heat. Add garlic and onion; cook, stirring, for 5 minutes or until onion is softened. Stir in cumin, cinnamon and hot pepper flakes; cook, stirring, for 1 minute. Stir in squash, chickpeas, lentils, tomatoes, broth, salt and pepper; bring to a boil. Reduce heat and simmer, stirring occasionally, for 20 minutes to blend the flavors. Let cool completely.

2. Divide soup evenly among jars and top with basil. Seal jars and refrigerate for up to 4 days.

3. When ready to serve, remove lid and microwave on High for 1 minute or until warmed through.

Citrus Halibut with Dill Rice

If you're looking for a hearty but healthy meal, this is it. Plus, it's easy to make and easy to take along.

Tips

You can use ready-to-use chicken broth instead of water to make more flavorful rice.

Use caution when removing the jar from the microwave, as the glass could be quite hot.

- Preheat broiler, with rack set 5 to 6 inches (12.5 to 15 cm) below the heat source
- Baking sheet, lined with foil
- 1-pint (500 mL) wide-mouth mason jar

1 cup	water	250 mL
½ cup	long-grain white rice	125 mL
½ tsp	salt, divided	2 mL
¼ cup	finely chopped fresh dill	60 mL
1 tsp	butter	5 mL
1 tsp	grated lemon zest	5 mL
1 tbsp	freshly squeezed lemon juice	15 mL
1 tbsp	olive oil	15 mL
½ tsp	freshly ground black pepper	2 mL
6 oz	skinless halibut fillet	175 g
1 tbsp	chopped fresh basil	15 mL
1	lemon wedge	1

1. In a medium saucepan, bring water to a boil over high heat. Stir in rice and half the salt, reduce heat to low, cover and simmer for 20 minutes or until rice is tender and water is absorbed. Remove from heat and stir in dill and butter, fluffing rice with a fork. Let cool completely.

2. Meanwhile, in a small bowl, combine lemon zest, lemon juice, oil, pepper and the remaining salt. Rub over both sides of fish. Place fish on prepared baking sheet. Broil for about 8 minutes, checking often to make sure fish doesn't burn, until fish is opaque and flakes easily when tested with a fork. Let cool completely, then cut fish into two pieces.

3. Spoon rice into jar and top with fish pieces, basil and lemon wedge. Seal jar and refrigerate for up to 2 days.

4. When ready to serve, remove lid and lemon wedge. Microwave jar on High for 1 minute or until warmed through. (Or remove jar from the refrigerator 20 minutes before serving and eat fish and rice at room temperature.) Squeeze the juice from the lemon wedge over top.

Portable Paella

Considered the national dish of Spain, paella is made with rice, chorizo, shrimp and chicken. This recipe is a deconstructed version, using similar flavors and layering them.

Tips

Traditional paella includes cooked mussels. If you want to add them, remove the cooked mussels from the shells and refrigerate overnight. Add them to the jar on top of the shrimp.

Use caution when removing the jar from the microwave, as the glass could be quite hot.

Cooked meat and shellfish, such as the chicken and shrimp in this recipe, should be eaten within 3 days of when they are cooked. If using leftover chicken and shrimp, make sure their total storage time does not exceed 3 days.

- 1-quart (1 L) wide-mouth mason jar

1 cup	water	250 mL
½ cup	long-grain white rice	125 mL
¼ tsp	salt	1 mL
4	saffron threads	4
1 tsp	butter	5 mL
1 tbsp	olive oil	15 mL
½ cup	sliced red onion	125 mL
1 cup	chopped seeded tomatoes	250 mL
¼ tsp	smoked paprika	1 mL
½ cup	cooked peas	125 mL
¼ cup	finely chopped dry-cured chorizo	60 mL
½ cup	cold shredded cooked chicken	125 mL
4	cold cooked medium shrimp	4
¼ cup	chopped fresh parsley	60 mL

1. In a medium saucepan, bring water to a boil over high heat. Stir in rice, salt and saffron, reduce heat to low, cover and simmer for 20 minutes or until rice is tender and water is absorbed. Remove from heat and stir in butter, fluffing rice with a fork. Let cool completely.

2. Meanwhile, in a medium skillet, heat oil over medium-high heat. Add onion and cook, stirring, for 5 minutes or until softened. Stir in tomatoes and paprika; cook, stirring, for 2 to 3 minutes or until tomato juice has evaporated. Let cool completely.

3. Layer onion mixture, rice, peas, chorizo, chicken, shrimp and parsley in jar. Seal jar and refrigerate for up to 1 day.

4. When ready to serve, remove lid and microwave on High for 3 minutes or until warmed through.

Pulled-Apart Chicken Parmesan

By now, you've likely figured out that I like to deconstruct recipes, making a meal suggestive of the original dish but without the time-consuming preparation. This is one of those recipes. Instead of breading the chicken and frying it (which you can still do, if you like), this recipe simply layers all the classic ingredients on top of each other.

**MAKES
1 SERVING**

Tips

If you use fried breaded chicken, slice it into strips before adding it to the jar.

Use caution when removing the jar from the microwave, as the glass could be quite hot.

Cooked meat, such as the chicken in this recipe, should be eaten within 3 days of when it is cooked. If using leftover chicken, make sure its total storage time does not exceed 3 days.

- Preheat oven to 350°F (180°C)
- Rimmed baking sheet, lined with foil
- 1-quart (1 L) wide-mouth mason jar

½ cup	dry bread crumbs	125 mL
¼ cup	freshly grated Parmesan cheese	60 mL
½ cup	tomato sauce	125 mL
¼ cup	chopped fresh basil	60 mL
1 cup	cold shredded cooked chicken	250 mL
¼ cup	shredded mozzarella cheese	60 mL

1. In a small bowl, combine bread crumbs and Parmesan cheese. Spread in an even layer on prepared baking sheet. Toast in preheated oven, stirring occasionally, for 10 minutes or until golden brown. Let cool completely.

2. Spoon tomato sauce into jar. Layer basil, chicken, mozzarella and toasted bread crumb mixture on top. Seal jar and refrigerate for up to 2 days.

3. When ready to serve, remove lid and microwave on High for 1 minute or until warmed through.

"Holiday Leftovers" Dinner

Leftovers make the best dinners, but why wait for the next holiday to make a "leftovers" feast? This meal uses a combination of store-bought favorites with homemade mashed potatoes so you can turn any day into a holiday. Of course, if you do have leftovers on hand, you can use them!

MAKES 2 SERVINGS

Tips

If you have leftover gravy, spoon it into each jar first, followed by chicken, thyme, cranberry sauce and mashed potatoes.

Use caution when removing the jar from the microwave, as the glass could be quite hot.

If serving two people at the same time, you can microwave both jars together, but increase the time by 30 seconds.

Cooked meat, such as the chicken or turkey in this recipe, should be eaten within 3 days of when it is cooked. If using leftover chicken or turkey, make sure its total storage time does not exceed 3 days.

- Rimmed baking sheet, lined with foil
- Ricer or potato masher
- Two 1-pint (500 mL) wide-mouth mason jars

4	small Yukon Gold potatoes, peeled and quartered	4
¼ cup	milk	60 mL
2 tbsp	butter	30 mL
¼ cup	cranberry sauce	60 mL
2 cups	cold shredded cooked chicken or turkey	500 mL
1 tbsp	chopped fresh thyme	15 mL

1. Place potatoes in a medium saucepan and cover with salted cold water. Bring to a boil over high heat. Boil for 15 to 20 minutes or until fork-tender.
2. Meanwhile, preheat oven to 350°F (180°C).
3. Drain potatoes and spread in an even layer on prepared baking sheet. Bake in preheated oven for 5 minutes to evaporate the water.
4. Run potatoes, one at a time, through the ricer and into a bowl (or mash potatoes in the bowl).
5. In a small saucepan, over medium-low heat, heat milk and butter until butter is melted. Gradually add warmed milk mixture to the potatoes, stirring to combine. Let cool completely.
6. Layer cranberry sauce, chicken, thyme and mashed potatoes in jars, dividing evenly. Seal jars and refrigerate for up to 3 days.
7. When ready to serve, remove lid and microwave on High for 1 minute or until warmed through.

Black Bean Chili with Chorizo

This terrific chili takes no time at all, is full of fiber and can be prepared several days in advance.

Tips

Experiment with different toppings for this chili. Try chopped avocado, sour cream or chopped tomatoes.

Use caution when removing the jar from the microwave, as the glass could be quite hot.

If serving two people at the same time, you can microwave two jars together, but increase the time by 30 seconds. Do not microwave more than two jars simultaneously.

• **Four 1-pint (500 mL) wide-mouth mason jars**

1 tbsp	olive oil	15 mL
2	cloves garlic, finely chopped	2
1	small onion, finely chopped	1
2 tbsp	chili powder	30 mL
1 tsp	ground cumin	5 mL
1 tsp	smoked paprika	5 mL
1 tsp	salt	5 mL
2 cups	rinsed drained canned black beans	500 mL
2 cups	canned diced tomatoes, with juice	500 mL
1 cup	finely chopped dry-cured chorizo	250 mL
½ cup	finely chopped roasted red bell peppers (see tip, page 115)	125 mL
½ cup	ready-to-use chicken broth	125 mL
½ cup	chopped fresh cilantro	125 mL

1. In a large pot, heat oil over medium-high heat. Add garlic and onion; cook, stirring, for 1 to 2 minutes or until softened. Stir in chili powder, cumin, paprika and salt. Stir in beans, tomatoes, chorizo, roasted peppers and broth; bring to a boil. Reduce heat and simmer, stirring occasionally, for 20 to 30 minutes or until slightly thickened. Stir in cilantro and cook for 1 to 2 minutes to blend the flavors. Let cool completely.

2. Divide chili evenly among jars. Seal jars and refrigerate for up to 3 days.

3. When ready to serve, remove lid and microwave on High for 1 minute or until warmed through.

Variation

Black Bean Chili with Chicken: Replace the chorizo with 1 cup (250 mL) shredded cooked chicken.

Bacon Mac and Cheese

Mac and cheese is nothing new, but it's always good. Bacon kicks it up a notch in the yum department. Eight-ounce (250 mL) jars are the perfect portion size.

Tips

If you want to give your mac and cheese an extra bite, try stirring in 1 tbsp (15 mL) Dijon mustard with the cheese in step 5.

Use caution when removing the jar from the microwave, as the glass could be quite hot.

- Preheat oven to 400°F (200°C)
- Rimmed baking sheet, lined with foil
- Four 8-oz (250 mL) wide-mouth mason jars

½ cup	panko (Japanese bread crumbs)	125 mL
6	slices bacon	6
4 cups	salted water	1 L
2 cups	dried elbow macaroni	500 mL
1 cup	milk	250 mL
1 tbsp	butter	15 mL
1 tbsp	all-purpose flour	15 mL
1½ cups	shredded sharp (old) Cheddar cheese	375 mL
1 tsp	freshly grated black pepper	5 mL
1 tbsp	chopped fresh flat-leaf (Italian) parsley	15 mL

1. Spread panko on prepared baking sheet. Bake in preheated oven for about 5 minutes or until golden brown. Leaving oven on, transfer panko to a bowl and let cool completely.

2. Wipe any excess crumbs from foil and arrange bacon on baking sheet. Bake for 12 minutes or until crispy. Transfer to a plate lined with paper towels and let cool, then chop into small pieces.

3. Meanwhile, in a medium pot, bring salted water to a boil over high heat. Add pasta and boil, stirring occasionally, for 9 minutes or until firm to the bite. Drain and let cool completely.

4. In a small saucepan, warm milk over medium-low heat for 5 minutes.

5. In a medium saucepan, melt butter over medium heat. Whisk in flour and cook, whisking, for 1 minute to prevent lumps from forming. Gradually whisk in warmed milk until smooth; cook, whisking, for about 5 minutes or until slightly thickened. Whisk in cheese and pepper; cook, whisking, until cheese is melted and sauce is smooth. Fold in macaroni.

Tip

If serving two people at the same time, you can microwave two jars together, but increase the time by 30 seconds. Do not microwave more than two jars simultaneously.

6. Divide half the macaroni mixture evenly among jars, then layer half the bacon on top. Repeat layers. Let cool completely.

7. Stir parsley into toasted panko, then sprinkle on top of bacon layer, dividing equally. Seal jars and refrigerate for up to 3 days.

8. When ready to serve, remove lid and microwave on High for 1 minute or until warmed through.

Variation

Lobster Mac and Cheese: Replace the chopped cooked bacon with $\frac{1}{2}$ cup (125 mL) chopped fresh or thawed frozen cooked lobster; add all of the lobster in the middle layer of the macaroni.

ploughman's Lunch

Originally created as a cold lunch that farmers could easily eat on their breaks, this meal has become a staple at most pubs. It's the perfect meal to pack in a jar, but don't pack it tightly — you'll want to be able to remove the items easily and assemble them on a plate for serving.

Tips

There are no rules to a ploughman's lunch. Experiment with different ingredients, such as pâté, hard-cooked eggs, cured meats and pickled vegetables.

Savory jams are another great addition to a ploughman's lunch. Pack jam separately in a 4-oz (125 mL) jar.

- 1-pint (500 mL) mason jar

½ cup	sliced apple	125 mL
1 tsp	freshly squeezed lemon juice	5 mL
6	gherkin pickles	6
4	slices sharp (old) Cheddar cheese	4
½ cup	sliced salami rounds	125 mL
¼ cup	niçoise or other olives	60 mL
4	crackers	4

1. Place apple slices in a bowl and drizzle with lemon juice, tossing to coat.
2. Layer pickles, cheese, salami, apples and olives in jar. Place a parchment paper round on top of the olives and top with crackers. Seal jar and refrigerate for up to 2 days.
3. When ready to serve, remove the ingredients and assemble them on a plate.

Southern BBQ Dinner

This cheater version of a pulled-pork sandwich is for those days when you wish you had a barbecue joint near your home.

Tips

Bread and butter pickles are often the pickle of choice when it comes to Southern barbecue, but the tart taste of dill pickles works well too. You decide.

Use caution when removing the jar from the microwave, as the glass could be quite hot.

If serving two people at the same time, you can microwave both jars together, but increase the time by 30 seconds.

- Preheat oven to 425°F (220°C)
- Rimmed baking sheet, lined with foil
- Two 1-quart (1 L) wide-mouth mason jars

1 cup	barbecue sauce	250 mL
1 lb	pork tenderloin, trimmed of fat and silverskin	500 g
¼ cup	chopped fresh flat-leaf (Italian) parsley	60 mL
2 tsp	granulated sugar	10 mL
1 tsp	salt	5 mL
1 tsp	freshly ground black pepper	5 mL
¾ cup	mayonnaise	175 mL
2 tbsp	apple cider vinegar	30 mL
4 cups	coleslaw mix	1 L
1 cup	drained canned baked beans	250 mL
½ cup	chopped sweet pickles	125 mL
1 cup	potato chips (optional)	250 mL

1. Set ½ cup (125 mL) of the barbecue sauce aside. Place pork on prepared baking sheet and brush liberally with the remaining barbecue sauce. Roast in preheated oven for 25 minutes or until an instant-read thermometer inserted in the thickest part of the tenderloin registers 145°F (63°C) for medium-rare. Remove from oven, tent with foil and let rest for 5 to 10 minutes.

2. Cut tenderloin crosswise into 8 chunks, then shred meat with two forks or your hands. Add pork to a large bowl, add the remaining barbecue sauce and toss to coat. Let cool completely.

3. In a medium bowl, whisk together parsley, sugar, salt, pepper, mayonnaise and vinegar. Stir in coleslaw until well combined.

4. Layer baked beans, pork, coleslaw and pickles in jars, dividing evenly. Seal jars and refrigerate for up to 3 days.

5. When ready to serve, remove lid and microwave on High for 3 minutes or until warmed through. Serve topped with potato chips, if desired.

Steak and Potatoes with Balsamic Tomatoes

Steak and potatoes are a classic pairing. This combo adds balsamic-glazed tomatoes for a new twist on the old staple.

MAKES 2 SERVINGS

Tips

You can use any sliced cooked cut of meat you like in place of the sliced grilled strip loin. Try beef flank steak, pork tenderloin or even sausage.

Reduced balsamic vinegar is fairly easy to find at grocery stores, but it's also easy to make your own. Pour 1 cup (250 mL) balsamic vinegar into a skillet and bring to a boil over medium-high heat. Reduce heat and simmer for 2 to 4 minutes or until thickened and syrupy. Remove from heat and let cool completely in the pan. It will continue to cook and thicken for a few minutes even off the heat.

- Preheat oven to 400°F (200°C)
- Rimmed baking sheet, lined with foil
- Two 1-pint (500 mL) mason jars
- Two 4-oz (125 mL) mason jars

1½ cups	sliced new potatoes	375 mL
1 cup	cherry tomatoes	250 mL
½ cup	thinly sliced red onion	125 mL
¼ cup	drained capers	60 mL
1 tbsp	freshly ground black pepper, divided	15 mL
½ tsp	salt, divided	2 mL
2 tbsp	reduced balsamic vinegar (see tip, at left)	30 mL
2 tbsp	olive oil, divided	30 mL
8 oz	boneless beef strip loin (New York strip) steak	250 g
1 tbsp	Dijon mustard	15 mL
1 cup	packed arugula	250 mL

1. In a bowl, toss together potatoes, tomatoes, onion, capers, half each of the pepper and salt, vinegar and half the oil. Spread in a single layer on prepared baking sheet. Bake in preheated oven for 25 minutes or until vegetables are caramelized. Let cool completely.

2. Meanwhile, preheat barbecue grill to medium-high. Brush both sides of steak with the remaining oil and season with the remaining pepper and salt. Grill steak for 4 to 5 minutes or until char marks appear on the bottom or steak is golden brown. Turn steak over and grill for 3 to 5 minutes for medium-rare, or to desired doneness. Remove from heat and let rest for 5 minutes, then slice across the grain into strips. Let cool completely.

Tips

Use caution when removing the jar from the microwave, as the glass could be quite hot.

If serving two people at the same time, you can microwave both 1-pint (500 mL) jars together, but increase the time by 30 seconds.

3. Layer potato mixture and steak in the 1-pint (500 mL) jars, dividing evenly. Dollop mustard on top. Seal jars and refrigerate for up to 3 days.

4. Divide arugula evenly between the 4-oz (125 mL) jars. Seal jars and refrigerate for up to 3 days.

5. When ready to serve, remove lid from 1-pint (500 mL) jar and microwave on High for 1 minute or until warmed through. Arrange steak and potato mixture on a plate and top with arugula.

Polenta Bolognese

This is an incredibly comforting meal — homemade Italian food at its best.

Tips

You can serve this topped with arugula and a drizzle of olive oil, but it's really just as good all on its own.

This dish works great with meatballs as well. Omit the ground beef from the sauce in step 1. Top the polenta with 3 cold cooked small meatballs, sauce, cheese, parsley and basil.

Use caution when removing the jar from the microwave, as the glass could be quite hot.

If serving two people at the same time, you can microwave both jars together, but increase the time by 30 seconds.

- **Two 1-quart (1 L) wide-mouth mason jars**

2 tbsp	olive oil	30 mL
½ cup	finely chopped onion	125 mL
¼ cup	finely chopped celery	60 mL
¼ cup	finely chopped carrots	60 mL
1	clove garlic, finely chopped	1
8 oz	lean ground beef	250 g
1 cup	canned diced tomatoes, with juice	250 mL
1 tbsp	chopped fresh oregano	15 mL
1 tsp	salt	5 mL
1 cup	ready-to-use chicken broth	250 mL
1 cup	heavy or whipping (35%) cream or milk	250 mL
½ cup	instant polenta	125 mL
2 tbsp	freshly grated Parmesan cheese, divided	30 mL
1 tsp	freshly ground black pepper	5 mL
1 tbsp	butter	15 mL
2 tbsp	chopped fresh flat-leaf (Italian) parsley	30 mL
1 tbsp	chopped fresh basil	15 mL

1. In a large saucepan, heat oil over medium-high heat. Add onion and cook, stirring, for 4 minutes. Add celery, carrots and garlic; cook, stirring, for 5 minutes or until softened. Add beef and cook, breaking it up with a spoon, for 7 to 10 minutes or until no longer pink. Stir in tomatoes, oregano and salt; reduce heat and simmer, stirring occasionally, for 10 minutes to blend the flavors. Let cool completely.

2. In a medium saucepan, bring broth and cream to a boil over medium-low heat. Add polenta, whisking constantly to prevent clumping. Reduce heat and simmer, whisking constantly, for about 3 minutes or until all of the liquid is absorbed. Remove from heat and stir in half the cheese, pepper and butter. Let cool completely.

3. Divide polenta evenly between jars and top with Bolognese sauce, the remaining cheese, parsley and basil. Seal jars and refrigerate for up to 3 days.

4. When ready to serve, remove lid and microwave on High for 1 minute or until warmed through.

Hummus, Lamb, Pine Nuts and Parsley

I first intended this dish as an appetizer, but it's hearty enough to eat as a meal. Serve it with a side salad for dinner or enjoy it as is.

Tips

To toast pine nuts, spread them in a single layer on a baking sheet. Toast in a 450°F (230°C) oven for 5 to 10 minutes, stirring occasionally, until golden brown. Let cool completely.

Use caution when removing the jar from the microwave, as the glass could be quite hot.

If serving two people at the same time, you can microwave both 4-oz (125 mL) jars together, but increase the time by 30 seconds.

- Two 4-oz (125 mL) mason jars
- Two 1-pint (500 mL) wide-mouth mason jars

1 tbsp	olive oil, divided	15 mL
8 oz	lean ground lamb	250 g
1 tsp	salt	5 mL
1 cup	hummus	250 mL
1 tsp	ground cinnamon	5 mL
1 tsp	smoked paprika	5 mL
¼ cup	chopped fresh flat-leaf (Italian) parsley	60 mL
2 tbsp	toasted pine nuts (see tip, at left)	30 mL
10	crackers	10

1. In a medium skillet, heat half the oil over medium-high heat. Add lamb and cook, breaking it up with a spoon, for 5 to 7 minutes or until no longer pink. Add the remaining oil and cook, stirring, until lamb is crispy. Stir in salt. Let cool completely.

2. Divide lamb evenly between 4-oz (125 mL) jars. Seal jars and refrigerate for up to 2 days.

3. Spoon hummus into 1-pint (500 mL) jars, dividing evenly, and sprinkle with cinnamon and paprika. Top with parsley and pine nuts, dividing evenly. Place a parchment paper round on top of the pine nuts and top with crackers. Seal jars and refrigerate for up to 2 days.

4. When ready to serve, remove lid from the lamb and microwave on High for 1 minute or until warmed through.

5. Remove the parchment paper and crackers from the hummus jar. Add warm lamb to the jar and serve with crackers.

Shepherd's Pie with Lamb and Wilted Spinach

This version of classic shepherd's pie layers wilted spinach between the meat and the potatoes. If spinach is not your thing, substitute any vegetable you prefer.

**MAKES
2 SERVINGS**

Tip

You can substitute lean ground chicken or beef for the lamb in this recipe.

- Rimmed baking sheet, lined with foil
- Ricer or potato masher
- Two 1-quart (1 L) wide-mouth mason jars

4	small Yukon Gold potatoes, peeled and quartered	4
¼ cup	milk	60 mL
2 tbsp	butter	30 mL
2 tbsp	olive oil, divided	30 mL
¼ cup	finely chopped onion	60 mL
8 oz	lean ground lamb	250 g
1 tsp	freshly ground black pepper	5 mL
½ tsp	salt, divided	2 mL
1 tbsp	finely chopped garlic	15 mL
1 tsp	hot pepper flakes	5 mL
3 cups	baby spinach	750 mL

1. Place potatoes in a medium saucepan and cover with salted cold water. Bring to a boil over high heat. Boil for 15 to 20 minutes or until fork-tender.
2. Meanwhile, preheat oven to 350°F (180°C).
3. Drain potatoes and spread in an even layer on prepared baking sheet. Bake in preheated oven for 5 minutes to evaporate the water.
4. Run potatoes, one at a time, through the ricer and into a bowl (or mash potatoes in the bowl).
5. In a small saucepan over medium-low heat, heat milk and butter until butter is melted. Gradually add warmed milk mixture to the potatoes, stirring to combine. Let cool completely.

Tips

Use caution when removing the jar from the microwave, as the glass could be quite hot.

If serving two people at the same time, you can microwave both jars together, but increase the time by 30 seconds.

6. In a medium skillet, heat half the oil over medium-high heat. Add onion and cook, stirring, for 3 minutes. Add lamb and cook, breaking it up with a spoon, for 5 to 7 minutes or until no longer pink. Stir in pepper and half the salt. Drain off any excess fat and let cool completely.

7. In a large skillet, heat the remaining oil over medium-low heat. Add garlic and hot pepper flakes; cook, stirring, for 1 minute. Add spinach and cook, stirring, for 1 minute. Add the remaining salt and cook, stirring, for 1 minute or until spinach is wilted and coated with garlic. Let cool completely.

8. Layer lamb mixture, spinach mixture and mashed potatoes in jars, dividing evenly. Seal jars and refrigerate for up to 3 days.

9. When ready to serve, remove lid on jar and microwave on High for 1 minute or until warmed through.

Dressings

Classic Vinaigrette, Done Six Ways

A vinaigrette is light-tasting and easy to make, and you can alter the flavor with a few fresh ingredients. Here are six variations on the classic.

MAKES ¾ TO 1⅓ CUPS (175 TO 325 ML)

Tip

Reduced balsamic vinegar is fairly easy to find at grocery stores, but it's also easy to make your own. Pour 1 cup (250 mL) balsamic vinegar into a skillet and bring to a boil over medium-high heat. Reduce heat and simmer for 2 to 4 minutes or until thickened and syrupy. Remove from heat and let cool completely in the pan. It will continue to cook and thicken for a few minutes even off the heat.

- 8-oz or 1-pint (250 or 500 mL) mason jar

Basic Vinaigrette

½ cup	extra virgin olive oil	125 mL
¼ cup	white wine vinegar	60 mL
1 tsp	Dijon mustard	5 mL
¼ tsp	salt	1 mL
¼ tsp	freshly ground black pepper	1 mL

1. In an 8-oz (250 mL) jar, combine oil, vinegar, mustard, salt and pepper. Seal jar and shake well. Makes about ¾ cup (175 mL).

Balsamic Vinaigrette

½ cup	extra virgin olive oil	125 mL
¼ cup	balsamic or reduced balsamic vinegar (see tip, at left)	60 mL
¼ tsp	kosher salt	1 mL
¼ tsp	freshly ground black pepper	1 mL

1. In an 8-oz (250 mL) jar, combine oil, vinegar, salt and pepper. Seal jar and shake well. Makes about ¾ cup (175 mL).

Italian Vinaigrette

½ tsp	minced garlic	2 mL
1¼ tsp	finely chopped fresh flat-leaf (Italian) parsley	6 mL
¼ tsp	kosher salt	1 mL
¼ tsp	freshly ground black pepper	1 mL
Pinch	hot pepper flakes	Pinch
½ cup	extra virgin olive oil	125 mL
¼ cup	red wine vinegar	60 mL
1 tsp	Dijon mustard	5 mL

1. In an 8-oz (250 mL) jar, combine garlic, parsley, salt, pepper, hot pepper flakes, oil, vinegar and mustard. Seal jar and shake well. Makes about ¾ cup (175 mL).

Tip

The classic vinaigrettes can be stored in the refrigerator for up to 1 week, with the exception of the Italian Vinaigrette, which can be stored for up to 3 days (to store longer, omit the garlic or use a pinch of dried granulated garlic or garlic powder instead of fresh).

Herb Vinaigrette

1 tsp	finely chopped shallots	5 mL
1 tsp	chopped fresh parsley	5 mL
1 tsp	chopped fresh basil	5 mL
1/2 tsp	fresh thyme	2 mL
1/4 tsp	kosher salt	1 mL
1/4 tsp	freshly ground black pepper	1 mL
1/2 cup	extra virgin olive oil	125 mL
1/4 cup	white wine vinegar	60 mL
1 tsp	Dijon mustard	5 mL

1. In an 8-oz (250 mL) jar, combine shallots, parsley, basil, thyme, salt, pepper, oil, vinegar and mustard. Seal jar and shake well. Makes about 3/4 cup (175 mL).

Lemon Poppy Seed Vinaigrette

2 tsp	poppy seeds	10 mL
1/4 tsp	kosher salt	1 mL
1/4 tsp	freshly ground black pepper	1 mL
3/4 cup	extra virgin olive oil	175 mL
1/3 cup	freshly squeezed lemon juice	75 mL
1/4 cup	unseasoned rice vinegar	60 mL
1 tbsp	liquid honey	15 mL

1. In a 1-pint (500 mL) jar, combine poppy seeds, salt, pepper, oil, lemon juice, vinegar and honey. Seal jar and shake well. Makes about 1 1/3 cups (325 mL).

Orange and Fennel Vinaigrette

1/4 cup	finely chopped fennel bulb	60 mL
2 tbsp	finely chopped fennel fronds	30 mL
1/4 tsp	kosher salt	1 mL
1/4 tsp	freshly ground black pepper	1 mL
1/2 cup	extra virgin olive oil	125 mL
2 tsp	grated orange zest	10 mL
1/4 cup	freshly squeezed orange juice	60 mL
1 tsp	liquid honey	5 mL

1. In an 8-oz (250 mL) jar, combine fennel bulb, fennel fronds, salt, pepper, oil, orange zest, orange juice and honey. Seal jar and shake well. Makes about 1 cup (250 mL).

Sweet Balsamic Vinaigrette

Add this simple and slightly sweet dressing to just about any lettuce-based salad. It works particularly well with Italian-inspired salads.

MAKES ABOUT ½ CUP (125 ML)

Tip

Store in the refrigerator for up to 3 days.

- 4-oz (125 mL) mason jar

1	clove garlic, minced	1
1 tsp	packed light brown sugar	5 mL
	Salt and freshly ground black pepper	
7 tbsp	extra virgin olive oil	105 mL
2 tbsp	reduced balsamic vinegar (see tip, page 164)	30 mL
1 tsp	Dijon mustard	5 mL

1. In jar, combine garlic, brown sugar, salt and pepper to taste, oil, vinegar and mustard. Seal jar and shake well.

Citrus Vinaigrette

The combination of freshly squeezed citrus juice and fresh basil and cilantro make this dressing a mouthwatering addition to any light, lettuce-based salad.

MAKES ABOUT ¾ CUP (175 ML)

Tip

Store in the refrigerator for up to 3 days.

- 8-oz (250 mL) mason jar

1	clove garlic, minced	1
1 tbsp	grated gingerroot	15 mL
1 tbsp	chopped fresh basil	15 mL
1 tbsp	chopped fresh cilantro	15 mL
¼ cup	freshly squeezed orange juice	60 mL
2 tbsp	extra virgin olive oil	30 mL
2 tbsp	unseasoned rice vinegar	30 mL
1 tbsp	liquid honey	15 mL
2 tsp	freshly squeezed lemon juice	10 mL
1 tsp	sesame oil	5 mL

1. In jar, combine garlic, ginger, basil, cilantro, orange juice, olive oil, vinegar, honey, lemon juice and sesame oil. Seal jar and shake well.

Greek Vinaigrette

This classic is primarily used for Greek salad, but it will work with just about anything.

Tips

Store in the refrigerator for up to 3 days.

If you have fresh oregano on hand, use 2 tbsp (30 mL) chopped fresh oregano in place of the dried. It will heighten the flavor of the salad.

* 1-pint (500 mL) mason jar

2	cloves garlic, minced	2
1 tbsp	dried oregano	15 mL
1 tsp	salt	5 mL
1 tsp	freshly ground black pepper	5 mL
1 tsp	granulated sugar	5 mL
½ cup	extra virgin olive oil	125 mL
¼ cup	red wine vinegar	60 mL
1 tbsp	freshly squeezed lemon juice	15 mL

1. In jar, combine garlic, oregano, salt, pepper, sugar, oil, vinegar and lemon juice. Seal jar and shake well.

Sesame Dressing

This is a great go-to for Asian-inspired salads. It works well with both noodle- and lettuce-based salads. I adore the distinct nutty flavor of sesame oil. When partnered with fresh ginger, it's just awesome.

Tip

Store in the refrigerator for up to 3 days.

* 8-oz (250 mL) mason jar

2 tbsp	chopped fresh cilantro	30 mL
2 tsp	finely chopped shallot	10 mL
1 tsp	grated gingerroot	5 mL
¼ cup	unseasoned rice vinegar	60 mL
3 tbsp	extra virgin olive oil	45 mL
3 tbsp	sesame oil	45 mL

1. In jar, combine cilantro, shallots, ginger, vinegar, olive oil and sesame oil. Seal jar and shake well.

Sweet Heat Dressing

This dressing is inspired by the sweet chile dipping sauce that is served with rice-paper spring rolls. It's sweet and tangy, with the perfect amount of heat. It's superb with Asian-inspired noodle salads.

MAKES ABOUT ¾ CUP (175 ML)

Tip

Store in the refrigerator for up to 3 days.

- 8-oz (250 mL) mason jar

1	clove garlic, minced	1
2 tbsp	chopped fresh mint	30 mL
1 tbsp	finely grated carrot	15 mL
2 tbsp	granulated sugar	30 mL
¼ tsp	hot pepper flakes	1 mL
¼ cup	fish sauce (nam pla)	60 mL
¼ cup	unseasoned rice vinegar	60 mL
2 tbsp	freshly squeezed lime juice	30 mL

1. In jar, combine garlic, mint, carrot, sugar, hot pepper flakes, fish sauce, vinegar and lime juice. Seal jar and shake well. Refrigerate for at least 2 hours before serving.

Honey Mustard Dressing

It's amazing how so few ingredients can taste so good. You could use this dressing on any salad. It's simple, fresh and flavorful. Flavored honeys, such as lavender or thyme, would work well, too.

MAKES ABOUT ⅔ CUP (150 ML)

Tip

Store in the refrigerator for up to 3 days.

- 8-oz (250 mL) mason jar

6 tbsp	extra virgin olive oil	90 mL
2 tbsp	white wine vinegar	30 mL
1 tbsp	liquid honey	15 mL
2 tsp	smooth Dijon mustard	10 mL
1 tsp	freshly ground black pepper	5 mL
½ tsp	salt	2 mL

1. In jar, combine oil, vinegar, honey, mustard, pepper and salt. Seal jar and shake well.

Lemon Dijon Dressing

Dijon mustard not only adds a bit of heat to this dressing, it also acts as a thickener. If you prefer to leave the garlic out, the dressing will still work well.

MAKES ABOUT ½ CUP (125 ML)

Tip

Store in the refrigerator for up to 3 days.

* 4-oz (125 mL) mason jar

1	clove garlic, minced	1
	Salt and freshly ground black pepper	
6 tbsp	extra virgin olive oil	90 mL
2 tbsp	freshly squeezed lemon juice	30 mL
1 tsp	Dijon mustard	5 mL

1. In jar, combine garlic, salt and pepper to taste, oil, lemon juice and mustard. Seal jar and shake well.

Lemon Tahini Dressing

If you're looking for a dressing with Middle Eastern flare, this is a great choice. Tahini can now be found at most grocery stores.

MAKES ABOUT 1 CUP (250 ML)

Tip

Store in the refrigerator for up to 3 days.

* 8-oz (250 mL) mason jar

1	clove garlic, minced	1
2 tbsp	chopped fresh flat-leaf (Italian) parsley	30 mL
1 tsp	salt	5 mL
⅛ tsp	cayenne pepper	0.5 mL
¼ cup	extra virgin olive oil	60 mL
3 tbsp	tahini	45 mL
2 tbsp	freshly squeezed lemon juice	30 mL
2 tbsp	water	30 mL

1. In jar, combine garlic, parsley, salt, cayenne, oil, tahini, lemon juice and water. Seal jar and shake well.

Avocado Lime Dressing

Avocados are the "it" ingredient these days. This dressing is great for salads, but it can also double as a dip for vegetables or poached shrimp.

**MAKES ABOUT
1½ CUPS
(375 ML)**

Tip

Store in the refrigerator for up to 3 days.

- Blender
- 1-pint (500 mL) mason jar

1	ripe avocado	1
1	clove garlic, roughly chopped	1
3 tbsp	packed fresh cilantro leaves	45 mL
½ tsp	granulated sugar	2 mL
½ tsp	salt	2 mL
2 tbsp	freshly squeezed lime juice	30 mL
2 tbsp	water	30 mL
1 tbsp	unseasoned rice vinegar	15 mL
6 tbsp	extra virgin olive oil	90 mL

1. In blender, combine avocado, garlic, cilantro, sugar, salt, lime juice, water and vinegar. With the motor running, through the feed tube, gradually add oil, processing until smooth. Pour into jar.

Blue Cheese and Chive Dressing

This is a great dressing to use on salads that contain steak or chicken. I like using it with the Steakhouse Salad (page 120) or the Classic Cobb Salad (page 114).

**MAKES ABOUT
1 CUP (250 ML)**

Tips

A soft blue cheese is not ideal for this recipe, as it will wilt lettuce leaves. Try a firmer cheese, such as Stilton, that holds together in larger chunks.

Store in the refrigerator for up to 3 days.

- 8-oz (250 mL) mason jar

1	clove garlic, minced	1
¼ cup	crumbled firm blue cheese	60 mL
2 tbsp	chopped fresh chives	30 mL
½ tsp	freshly ground black pepper	2 mL
½ tsp	salt	2 mL
½ cup	well-shaken buttermilk	125 mL
2 tbsp	freshly squeezed lemon juice	30 mL

1. In jar, combine garlic, cheese, chives, pepper, salt, buttermilk and lemon juice. Seal jar and shake well.

Cucumber Dill Dressing

Simple and fresh, this dressing is an amazing complement to fish. Try it with Roasted Salmon with Bibb Lettuce and Crispy Leeks (page 101) or any salad made with fish or shellfish.

(page 101)

MAKES ABOUT ¾ CUP (175 ML)

Tip

Store in the refrigerator for up to 3 days.

- 8-oz (250 mL) mason jar

1	clove garlic, minced	1
3 tbsp	grated cucumber, with juice	45 mL
2 tbsp	chopped fresh dill	30 mL
½ cup	sour cream	125 mL
2 tsp	freshly squeezed lemon juice	10 mL

1. In jar, whisk together garlic, cucumber, dill, sour cream and lemon juice. Seal jar and refrigerate for at least 2 hours before serving.

Ranch Dressing

Most of us have had ranch dressing from a bottle, but this homemade creamy dressing, made with fresh herbs, has a vastly heightened flavor. You don't have to limit it to Cobb salad; it works with any salad with crunchy vegetables or heartier lettuce.

MAKES ABOUT ¾ CUP (175 ML)

Tips

Store in the refrigerator for up to 3 days.

This dressing can also be used as a dip, and if desired you can double the recipe.

- 8-oz (250 mL) mason jar

1 tbsp	minced shallot	15 mL
1 tsp	minced garlic	5 mL
1 tsp	chopped fresh parsley	5 mL
1 tsp	chopped fresh dill	5 mL
	Salt and freshly ground black pepper	
½ cup	well-shaken buttermilk	125 mL
2 tbsp	freshly squeezed lemon juice	30 mL
1 tbsp	plain yogurt	15 mL

1. In jar, combine shallot, garlic, parsley, dill, salt and pepper to taste, buttermilk, lemon juice and yogurt. Seal jar and shake well.

Thousand Island Dressing

Thousand Island dressing gets a bit of a bad rap, being seen as less sophisticated than lighter vinaigrettes. Fancy it's not, but delicious it is. Try it on top of a wedge of iceberg lettuce, or on any salad that requires a creamier dressing, such as the BLT Salad (page 52) or Classic Cobb Salad (page 114).

MAKES ABOUT
¾ CUP (175 ML)

Tip

Store in the refrigerator for up to 3 days.

- 8-oz (250 mL) mason jar

2 tsp	granulated sugar	10 mL
⅛ tsp	salt	0.5 mL
⅛ tsp	freshly ground black pepper	0.5 mL
½ cup	mayonnaise	125 mL
2 tbsp	ketchup	30 mL
1 tbsp	white vinegar	15 mL
2 tsp	sweet relish	10 mL

1. In a small bowl, whisk together sugar, salt, pepper, mayonnaise, ketchup, vinegar and relish until smooth. Pour into jar.

Creamy Caesar Dressing

Everyone needs to have a good Caesar salad dressing at their disposal, and this one doesn't disappoint. And it's not just for Caesars — try it with a Cobb, chef or fish taco salad.

**MAKES ABOUT
1¼ CUPS
(300 ML)**

Tips

This recipe contains a raw egg. If you are concerned about the food safety of raw eggs, substitute a pasteurized egg in the shell or 3 tbsp (45 mL) pasteurized liquid whole eggs.

Store in the refrigerator for up to 3 days.

- Blender
- 1-pint (500 mL) mason jar

1	clove garlic, minced	1
1	large egg	1
2 tbsp	freshly squeezed lemon juice	30 mL
1 tbsp	white wine vinegar	15 mL
1 tsp	Dijon mustard	5 mL
½ tsp	Worcestershire sauce	2 mL
⅛ tsp	hot pepper sauce	0.5 mL
¾ cup	extra virgin olive oil	175 mL

1. In blender, combine garlic, egg, lemon juice, vinegar, mustard, Worcestershire sauce and hot pepper sauce. With the motor running, through the feed tube, gradually add oil, processing until smooth. Pour into jar.

Desserts

Cute and Clever Key Lime Pie

My favorite thing to do in a Florida airport is look at all the alligator paraphernalia and citrus products. A few years back, I got hooked on Key lime juice, and now I always pick up a bottle on my way home. It's a bit more tart than Persian lime juice, but it's perfect for tarts, fruit salads and marinades.

Tip

If you happen to have access to Key limes, by all means use grated Key lime zest and freshly squeezed juice. If you can't find bottled Key lime juice, substitute Persian lime juice.

- 8-oz (250 mL) mason jar

¼ cup	graham cracker crumbs	60 mL
1 tsp	melted unsalted butter	5 mL
1 tbsp	granulated sugar	15 mL
¼ cup	cream cheese, softened	60 mL
2 tbsp	sour cream	30 mL
1 tbsp	grated lime zest	15 mL
2 tbsp	Key lime juice	30 mL
¼ cup	blueberries	60 mL

1. In a small bowl, combine graham cracker crumbs and butter.
2. In a medium bowl, whisk together sugar, cream cheese, sour cream, lime zest and lime juice.
3. Press graham cracker mixture firmly into bottom of jar. Layer cream cheese mixture and blueberries on top. Seal jar and refrigerate for up to 2 days.

Variation

Chocolate Key Lime Pie: Drizzle 1 tbsp (15 mL) melted chocolate on top of the cream cheese mixture in the jar. Chill, then top with blueberries or raspberries.

No-Bake Raspberry Tart

This mini version of a simple no-bake tart is easy to take to work as an afternoon snack, but you could also make several portions to serve as individual desserts at a party.

**MAKES
1 SERVING**

Tip

Any berries will look beautiful on top of this dessert — try blueberries, blackberries or sliced strawberries, and match the jam flavor to the berries. Concentric circles of pomegranate seeds also make a fun topping.

• 8-oz (250 mL) mason jar

¼ cup	graham cracker crumbs	60 mL
1 tsp	melted butter	5 mL
1 tbsp	granulated sugar	15 mL
¼ cup	cream cheese, softened	60 mL
2 tbsp	sour cream	30 mL
1 tbsp	freshly squeezed lemon juice	15 mL
¼ cup	raspberries	60 mL
2 tbsp	raspberry jam	30 mL

1. In a small bowl, combine graham cracker crumbs and butter.
2. In a medium bowl, whisk together sugar, cream cheese, sour cream and lemon juice.
3. Press graham cracker mixture firmly into bottom of jar. Layer cream cheese mixture and raspberries on top.
4. Spoon jam into a small microwave-safe bowl and microwave on High for 30 seconds or until runny. Stir jam, then pour over berries. Let cool completely, then seal jar and refrigerate for at least 4 hours, until chilled, or for up to 2 days.

Variation

Chocolate Raspberry Tart: Drizzle 1 tbsp (15 mL) melted chocolate over the berries in place of the jam.

Petite Pumpkin Pies

This super-cute, festive dessert is also great as a midday treat.

Tip

This recipe also works well without the cream cheese layer. Just use the crust and the pumpkin mixture and serve as is or top with grated chocolate.

- Preheat oven to 350°F (180°C)
- Food processor
- Baking sheet, lined with parchment paper or foil
- Four 8-oz (250 mL) mason jars

½ cup	pecan halves	125 mL
½ cup	ginger snaps	125 mL
1 tbsp	softened unsalted butter	15 mL
¼ cup	granulated sugar	60 mL
1 tsp	ground cinnamon	5 mL
1 tsp	ground nutmeg	5 mL
1 tsp	ground cloves	5 mL
1 cup	pumpkin purée (not pie filling)	250 mL
2 tbsp	sour cream	30 mL
½ cup	heavy or whipping (35%) cream	125 mL
2 tbsp	confectioners' (icing) sugar	30 mL
½ cup	cream cheese, softened	125 mL
1 tsp	vanilla extract	5 mL

1. In food processor, pulse pecans and gingersnaps into crumbs. Add butter and pulse to combine.

2. Spread pecan mixture on prepared baking sheet. Bake in preheated oven for 5 minutes or until golden. Let cool completely.

3. In a medium bowl, combine granulated sugar, cinnamon, nutmeg, cloves, pumpkin and sour cream.

4. In a large bowl, using an electric mixer, whip cream until stiff peaks form. Beat in confectioners' sugar, cream cheese and vanilla.

5. Press pecan mixture firmly into bottom of jars, dividing evenly. Layer cream cheese mixture and pumpkin mixture on top, dividing evenly. Seal jars and refrigerate for at least 2 hours, until chilled, or for up to 2 days.

Teensy Apple Crisps

Apple crisp is one of the best desserts to make in the fall. It works plain, served with a dollop of whipped cream or warmed and topped with a scoop of ice cream. It's the perfect treat to take with you for lunch.

MAKES 4 SERVINGS

Tips

The key to the crumb topping is to use cold butter. It will make the crumble crunchy.

Every microwave is different. Test your apples after 1 minute; if they need more time, continue heating in 30-second intervals.

Use caution when removing the jar from the microwave, as the glass could be quite hot.

- Preheat oven to 350°F (180°C)
- Rimmed baking sheet, lined with parchment paper or foil
- Four 8-oz (250 mL) wide-mouth mason jars, greased

¼ cup	packed brown sugar	60 mL
¼ cup	quick-cooking rolled oats	60 mL
¼ cup	whole wheat flour	60 mL
3 tbsp	chopped praline pecans	45 mL
1 tbsp	ground cinnamon, divided	15 mL
3 tbsp	cold unsalted butter, cut into small pieces	45 mL
2 cups	chopped peeled apples	500 mL
1 tbsp	granulated sugar	15 mL
½ tsp	ground nutmeg	2 mL
1 tbsp	freshly squeezed lemon juice	15 mL
½ tsp	vanilla extract	2 mL

1. In a medium bowl, combine brown sugar, oats, flour, pecans and half the cinnamon. Using the back of a fork, press in butter. Using your hands, combine until mixture looks crumbly and sticks together. Spread evenly on prepared baking sheet.

2. Bake in preheated oven for 5 to 7 minutes or until golden brown. Let cool completely on pan on a wire rack.

3. Meanwhile, in a large bowl, toss apples with granulated sugar, the remaining cinnamon, nutmeg, lemon juice and vanilla.

4. Divide apple mixture evenly among prepared jars. Top with crumb mixture, dividing evenly. Microwave on High for 1 minute or until apples are tender. Let cool completely.

5. Sprinkle crumb topping over cooled apples, dividing evenly. Seal jars and refrigerate for up to 3 days.

6. Serve cold or remove lid and microwave on High for 1 minute or until warmed through.

Cherry Chocolate Crumble

This is a magical dessert. The cherries, chocolate crumble and dark chocolate work so beautifully together. I wish I could take credit for it, but my friend and food editor Jennifer MacKenzie gave me the idea. It's now my go-to dessert!

**MAKES
4 SERVINGS**

Tip
If you can't find dark chocolate chips, you can use shaved dark chocolate or bittersweet or milk chocolate chips instead.

- Preheat oven to 350°F (180°C)
- Rimmed baking sheet, lined with parchment paper or foil
- Four 8-oz (250 mL) wide-mouth mason jars, greased

¼ cup	packed brown sugar	60 mL
¼ cup	quick-cooking rolled oats	60 mL
¼ cup	whole wheat flour	60 mL
1 tbsp	unsweetened cocoa powder	15 mL
3 tbsp	cold unsalted butter, cut into small pieces	45 mL
3 cups	frozen sweet cherries, thawed	750 mL
1 tbsp	grated lemon zest	15 mL
1 tbsp	freshly squeezed lemon juice	15 mL
1 tbsp	dark chocolate chips	15 mL

1. In a medium bowl, combine brown sugar, oats, flour and cocoa powder. Using the back of a fork, press in butter. Using your hands, combine until mixture looks crumbly and sticks together. Spread evenly on prepared baking sheet.

2. Bake in preheated oven for 5 to 7 minutes or until golden brown. Let cool completely on pan on a wire rack.

3. Meanwhile, in a large bowl, combine cherries, lemon zest and lemon juice.

4. Divide cherry mixture evenly among prepared jars. Top with crumble mixture, dividing evenly. Microwave on High for 1 minute or until cherries are tender. Divide chocolate chips evenly among jars. Seal jars and refrigerate for up to 3 days.

5. Serve cold or remove lid and microwave on High for 1 minute or until warmed through.

Brownie Smothered in Chocolate

This indulgent dessert is hardly diet-worthy, but it is worth every bite.

Tip

The crusty parts of the brownies are excellent in this dessert, as they hold their crunch even after being buried in the whipped cream.

- 8-oz (250 mL) mason jar

¼ cup	heavy or whipping (35%) cream	60 mL
¼ cup	chopped brownies	60 mL
¼ cup	chocolate hazelnut spread	60 mL

1. In a medium bowl, using an electric mixer, whip cream until soft peaks form.
2. Pack brownies tightly in bottom of jar. Layer chocolate hazelnut spread and whipped cream on top. Seal jar and refrigerate for up to 2 days.

Variation

Chocolate Raspberry Brownies: Substitute an equal amount of mashed raspberries for the whipped cream.

Banana Bread Parfait

You could make this yummy dessert with any type of loaf, but banana is my favorite.

Tip

The dessert doesn't need it, but if you prefer a sweetened whipped cream, you can add 1 tsp (5 mL) granulated sugar to the whipped cream.

- 4-oz (125 mL) mason jar

¼ cup	heavy or whipping (35%) cream	60 mL
1	thick slice banana bread	1
½	banana, sliced	½
1 tbsp	chocolate chips	15 mL

1. In a medium bowl, using an electric mixer, whip cream until soft peaks form.
2. Place banana bread on a cutting board and invert the jar on top, pressing a round mark into the bread. Cut out the round and place in bottom of jar. (Enjoy the remaining banana bread as a snack.)
3. Layer whipped cream, banana and chocolate chips on top of banana bread. Seal jar and refrigerate for up to 1 day.

Variation

Caramel Banana Bread Parfait: Omit the chocolate chips and drizzle caramel sauce on top of the banana.

Pretty Macaron Pavlova

The success of the mason jar dessert is its simplicity. This one is super-easy to make. Be inventive and try different flavors of macarons and fruit. Crushed store-bought meringues work well too.

Tip

A pavlova is an Australian dessert made with meringue, whipped cream and fruit. You can easily recreate that here using store-bought meringues that you crush and layer on the bottom in place of the macarons. Use about 1/2 cup (125 mL) crushed meringues.

- 4-oz (125 mL) mason jar

1/4 cup	heavy or whipping (35%) cream	60 mL
3	raspberry macaron cookies (about 1 1/2 inches/4 cm in diameter), cut in half	3
8	raspberries	8

1. In a medium bowl, using an electric mixer, whip cream until soft peaks form.
2. Layer macarons, whipped cream and raspberries in jar. Seal jar and refrigerate for up to 1 day.

Variation

Chocolate Chip Pavlova: Substitute 2 chopped chocolate chip cookies (about 2 inches/5 cm in diameter) for the macarons.

Chocolate Hazelnut Mousse

This ingredient trio — hazelnuts, whipped cream and chocolate hazelnut spread — is heavenly!

Tip

To make this treat even more spectacular, add 1/4 cup (60 mL) sliced banana to the bottom of each jar before adding the whipped cream mixture.

- Food processor
- Four 4-oz (125 mL) mason jars

1 cup	hazelnuts	250 mL
1 cup	heavy or whipping (35%) cream	250 mL
1/2 cup	chocolate hazelnut spread	125 mL

1. In food processor, pulse hazelnuts into crumbs. Divide evenly among jars.
2. In a medium bowl, using an electric mixer, whip cream until stiff peaks form. Add chocolate hazelnut spread and whip to combine.
3. Divide whipped cream mixture evenly among jars. Seal jars and refrigerate for at least 2 hours, until chilled, or for up to 2 days.

Peanut Butter and Chocolate Dream

Nothing goes better together than peanut butter and chocolate, and this easy no-bake dessert showcases them to their best advantage.

Tips

You can purchase chocolate wafer crumbs or, in a small food processer or mini chopper, pulse 4 wafers to the consistency of fine crumbs.

For additional decadence, top the cream cheese mixture with whipped cream before adding the peanut butter cups.

- 8-oz (250 mL) mason jar

1 tbsp	granulated sugar	15 mL
¼ cup	cream cheese, softened	60 mL
1 tbsp	peanut butter	15 mL
1 tbsp	sour cream	15 mL
½ tsp	vanilla extract	2 mL
¼ cup	chocolate wafer crumbs (see tip, at left)	60 mL
¼ cup	broken chocolate peanut butter cups	60 mL

1. In a medium bowl, using an electric mixer, beat sugar, cream cheese, peanut butter, sour cream and vanilla until smooth.

2. Press wafer crumbs firmly into bottom of jar. Layer cream cheese mixture and peanut butter cups on top. Seal jar and refrigerate for at least 4 hours, until chilled, or for up to 3 days.

Banana S'mores

My husband has turned us into a camping family. It's not my idea of fun, but my three boys love it. I think their favorite part is eating s'mores. This is my jarred version of the campfire treat, and it happens to be my son Eddie's favorite dessert.

Tips

Heating this dessert in intervals helps you make sure it's not burning.

Use caution when removing the jar from the microwave, as the glass could be quite hot.

For traditional s'mores, simply omit the banana.

- 8-oz (250 mL) mason jar

¼ cup	graham cracker crumbs	60 mL
1 tsp	melted unsalted butter	5 mL
½	banana, sliced	½
¼ cup	mini marshmallows	60 mL
1 tbsp	chocolate chips	15 mL

1. In a small bowl, combine graham cracker crumbs and butter.
2. Press graham cracker mixture firmly into bottom of jar. Layer banana, marshmallows and chocolate chips on top. Seal jar and refrigerate for up to 2 days.
3. When ready to serve, remove lid and microwave on High in 15-second intervals until melted and bubbling.

Fruit Salad

There's nothing new about fruit salad, but prepping it in advance makes having it after lunch a no-brainer. Mix up the types of fruits you use to avoid a fruit rut.

Tips

For the best fit in the jar and an attractively uniform look, cut all the fruit into ¼-inch (0.5 cm) dice.

Squeeze a wedge of lemon or lime juice over your fruit salad before sealing the jar. It will keep your fruit looking fresh and add a hint of tartness.

- 8-oz (250 mL) mason jar

¼ cup	diced pineapple	60 mL
¼ cup	diced strawberries	60 mL
¼ cup	diced cantaloupe	60 mL
¼ cup	diced watermelon	60 mL

1. Layer pineapple, strawberries, melon and watermelon in jar. Seal jar and refrigerate for up to 3 days.

Variation

Fruit Salad with Ginger-Mint Dressing: Combine 1 tsp (5 mL) grated gingerroot, 1 tsp (5 mL) chopped fresh mint, 1 tbsp (15 mL) freshly squeezed lemon juice and 1 tsp (5 mL) liquid honey. Pour over fruit salad before sealing the jar.

Index

Library and Archives Canada Cataloguing in Publication

Linton, Tanya, author
150 best meals in a jar : salads, soups, rice bowls & more / Tanya Linton.

Includes index.
ISBN 978-0-7788-0528-1 (paperback)

1. Make-ahead cooking. 2. Quick and easy cooking. 3. Cookbooks.
I. Title. II. Title: One hundred fifty best meals in a jar.

TX652.L56 2016   641.5'55   C2015-908528-4